W9-CPC-042

Catholic Schools,
Public Education,
and
American Culture

MOST REVEREND JOHN B. MCDOWELL, PH.D

ACKNOWLEDGEMENTS

My special gratitude to Reverend Monsignor Donald W. Kraus, Reverend Ronald Lawler, OFM, Cap., and Dr. Cornelius Murphy, Jr., who extended every possible assistance during the writing of this work. For their patience, insights, suggestions and wisdom, I am profoundly grateful. My special thanks to Sister Anna Mary Gibson, R.S.M., and Sister Mary Noel Kernan, S.C., who did outstanding work in making the manuscript readable. Finally to my faithful and competent secretary, Mildred E. Keenan, for her unbelievable and inexhaustible efforts on the word processor and printer. To these and so many others, I am eternally grateful.

Our Sunday Visitor Publishing Division
Our Sunday Visitor, Inc.
200 Noll Plaza
Huntingdon, IN 46750

ISBN: 0-87973-397-7
LCCCN: 99-76262
Cover Design by Karen A. Mesaros

Printed in the United States of America

Dedication:

MONSIGNOR THOMAS JOSEPH QUIGLEY, PH.D.
March 4, 1905 — December 26, 1960

Mentor • Teacher • Confidant
Inspiration • Friend

Table of Contents

Preface

Through a presentation of personal reminiscences and astute insight into the legal and sociological history of education in America, Bishop McDowell in his book, Catholic Schools, Public Education, and American Culture, has produced a work of exceptional worth. Asserting that nothing gives better insight into the culture of a nation than the quality of its education system, Bishop McDowell demonstrates the significance of the contribution made by Catholic education in America. In the late twentieth century that contribution continues to be both notable and, in many quarters, contentious.

From the earliest Catholic schools in Maryland and New Orleans, founded by the Jesuit Fathers and the Ursuline Sisters respectively, to the present day parochial elementary and secondary schools, the contribution made by Catholic education has made a mark on the formation of education in our country in spite of considerable opposition. These obstacles have arisen from both civil court decisions and from bigotry with which those who embrace the Catholic faith in our nation have occasionally had to contend. The obstacles have stemmed from state legislatures mandating compulsory attendance only at public schools (Pierce v. Society of Sisters) to the opposition mounted by the Ku Klux Klan. Bishop McDowell's writing demonstrates that the recent controversies concerning school choice and a voucher system in our nation are continuing aspects of this history. Bishop McDowell ably demonstrates that the Catholic educational enterprise has met and surmounted these obstacles.

The role that education, and especially Catholic education, has played in the formation of values and morality in our country cannot be understated. Bishop McDowell focuses not only on the Catholic culture as contributing to values formation but goes deeper by calling attention to that "classroom" of the family in which the most important lessons are first taught. By focusing on the most basic unit of our culture the reader is made aware of the strong connection between what is held as sacred within our families and supported through Catholic education. Parental responsibilities for the spiritual formation at home and in the formal efforts of the classroom are manifestly linked in the efforts of Catholic educators. Bishop McDowell recognizes the importance of those educators. Saint Elizabeth Ann Seton, Blessed Katharine Drexel, and Father Michael McGivney are examples of educators and Catholics who, despite opposition, have been able to make known the teaching of the Gospel.

The efforts involved in Catholic education require the use of resources, both personal and communal; commitment from individuals and from the Church in America. Bishop McDowell has written of the significance and the benefits of

Catholic education in the United States. His work offers a twofold benefit for the reader. One is able to grasp a sense of history – personal and national – through Bishop McDowell's writings while at the same time gaining an appreciation for the significant contributions that Catholic education has made and continues to make in our country.

Anthony Cardinal Bevilacqua
Archbishop of Philadelphia

Introduction

Many kinds of reasons drove people to undertake the hazardous journey to the new world. The ocean voyage sometimes took many. It was itself surrounded with danger, and led people to a land filled with perils. Nevertheless immigrants were highly motivated, and they found the adventure a great challenge.

Over the years they arrived in enormous numbers. Some came because their government sent them. Others came for more personal reasons, often with hopes of escaping persecution, either religious or political. Many came out of a spirit of adventure; they wanted to be part of building a new world. Finally many came for heroic reasons. They were trying to do something important for their church or their homeland, and so they came with the hope of serving their country in grand ways, or to bring their faith to a land largely yet unevangelized.

Whatever the special reasons of each, all were inspired, it seems, by the hope that there would be something better rather than merely different in the new land. They sought a better place to live, or a better form of government, or a better home to raise their families. They cherished the hope that in the new land, unburdened by the ingrained injustices of the world left behind them, they might attain greater freedom, fuller justice, and more peace. In this land their children could be brought up and educated in ways that would be full of promise for the future, and a bracing support of all they held most dear.

The new world attracted people of every background. At first they came from the more adventurous nations: Spain, Italy, France, and England. These great nations sought new lands to expand the possibilities for their homeland. They wished to have colonies, and new raw materials which would bring greater wealth and a richer life. Not a few were even inspired by the desire to spread the faith of Christ, and to give the faith a more promising space in which to grow.

But the new world was not an easy undertaking for anyone. On the contrary, immigrants faced grave difficulties, not only in getting to America, but in making it into something livable. Homes had to be built; new roads were needed through wilderness, and rivers had to be utilized to provide new and better ways of transportation. Wild lands had to be subdued, then prepared, plowed and planted, if people were to survive. Natives of the land, through an easy mistake called the "American" Indians, had to be dealt with and some understanding about co-existence in the new land negotiated with them. If any immigrants left their homeland simply to escape great problems, they soon learned that moving into a new world did not provide an easy solution.

Nevertheless, they came to America.

The amazing story of the growth and development of this nation has been told and retold many times and in a host of ways. Most people are well acquainted with the great periods of the history of the new country. In the periods of exploration brave men were sought so they could learn where they were and what the new land had to offer. In the many periods of immigrations brave souls risked their life to get to the new world and plant roots there. The colonial period had splendid accomplishments but was also a time of great hardship and sacrifice. Then came the struggle for the establishment of a new republic, when a band of colonials repudiated the thoughtless authority and cruel oppression of the English and began their own government and a country built on a new vision. Then, in quick succession, came the westward movement, the many conflicts with the native Americans, the urbanization of the country, the Industrial Revolution, the Gay Nineties, the great period of inventions, the World Wars, the scientific age, the period of technological advancement, the computer age, and the space age. What these immigrants, and their descendants, managed to accomplish in a short period of time was almost beyond belief.

Not every nation can boast of such a history. In a world grown weary with many burdens from a long past, this nation was created deliberately as something new. It wished to cast behind it the weariness of what was burdensome in the past, and build the nation not on the privileges and precedents of an unfair past, but on a faith, a philosophy and a vision they counted most precious. In a sense, this nation was built on a vision. It was shaped by a democratic faith, a conviction of the importance of every person, and of recognizing as superior not the claims of the rich and powerful, but the inalienable rights of each person, and the right of everyone to pursue happiness and a full life. Overwhelmingly they were convinced: God was guiding them into better things. The great seal of America bears an image of God, and a motto: "Annuit coeptis" ("He has approved what we have begun").

This nation has indeed made many mistakes, and it too is always in danger of growing old by forgetting its dream. But America in many ways remains a nation that much of the world seeks to become like: it is seen to have unique kinds of greatness, and even to be yet a very young nation. Certainly not all peoples love America, and there have been good reasons for many to be distressed at our arrogance and missteps. Yet few are unmoved by its history, and its hopes, which often reflect the hopes and dreams of much of the world.

Even the most tragic and cruel decisions America has made seem touched by the conviction that something new was being built here for mankind. The native peoples who inhabited this land before Europeans came here, the "Indians," were very badly treated.

The truth is, however, that immigrants never dreamt of coming here to establish a continuation of the native American way of life, or to enter into that way of life, or any old and wearied way of living. Surely we need to be ashamed of our treatment of the native American peoples. Those people were immensely different from the immigrants, and were not understood by them. They had their own way of life, their own history, their own ideals, hopes and aspirations. But the immigrants could not see some things, because they came to establish new ways of living, new places to live, and new ideals and hopes.

The ravaging of natives stands as a terrible reality in our national memory. The tragic inability of people, seeking to do good, to see and appreciate the importance of the ideals and persons they do not understand, will form a large background to this history of education and schools in America. Extremely unjust things can be done in the pursuit of a dream in hearts that do not see enough. Early Americans failed to realize some things they should have, because they were so intent on something else. They almost had to see America as a new nation and an entirely new hope. It was a new beginning. Millions of immigrants came to make everything new — to make a clean start. What one now beholds is the result of their determination and extraordinary effort. But for our treatment of the natives we found here, we are forever shamed.

This study clearly is not intended to be a rounded account of the many facets of American history. Its focus is on education in American schools, on something central to the shaping of the soul of this nation. We concentrate on three points: (1) the establishment and development of public education, of government-managed education in America; (2) the development of Catholic schools, and, to a lesser extent, of other religious schools; and (3) the development of the American culture that over the years affected so much the various ways of admitting the whole vision of America into its treatment of various kinds of schools.

AMERICAN PUBLIC EDUCATION

The education of young people in its schools is an immensely important factor in the forming and developing of any people or community. In America the public school system is considered by some to be the most American of all things. It is manifestly official, the only state-approved and -supported educational program in the nation. Some seem to think that a public school was built right off Plymouth Rock in the nation's earliest days, and that the founding fathers were all graduates of public schools. Many suppose that public education was the only kind of education fitting to this new world, so that it must have had an early and stable beginning, and have always been here for those who came to live in this land or were born here.

Such of course is not the case. Public education got off to a slow start in America, and for many years it was unclear what kind of schools the communities of that nation should support. The earliest American schools were religious schools, handing on faith and a vision and values as well as basic skills. Even when the first public schools were shaped, they were far more religious than public schools are these days. American public education for years groped its way by trial and error.

Only in the second half of the nineteenth century did public education begin to take on certain more stable characteristics. In the early twentieth century these characteristics began to solidify. Other options had been possible. But public schools became what they did through many kinds of influences. Not all these were popular and democratically decided choices. There was an immense influence from a modest number of scholars and leaders, like Horace Mann and John Dewey. There were judicial decisions of great importance from the Supreme Court. Only gradually did the public school become what now it is. The public school became more clearly defined during the second half of the twentieth century. The long period of formation lasted from the late eighteenth until the mid-twentieth centuries.

Of course, the public school can never be a static institution. The most influential philosopher of education in America, John Dewey, maintains that the first rule of life and education must be change. Publicly supported education became what it is by many changes. It may yet change in important ways.

In the beginning, school education in America was a patchwork consisting principally of parochial and independent schools. Practically every religious group immigrating into this country established its own community as soon as possible, which always included a school to teach children the group's way of life as well as their own religious vision and hopes. Among those groups were the Quakers, Lutherans, Moravians, Mennonites, Baptists, Dunkers, and, of course, the Catholics.

From the beginning new settlers felt compelled to instruct their children, not only in the basic skills of life, but in what life means and what is the context of our hope, the essence of life as they understood it.

AMERICAN CATHOLIC EDUCATION

The Catholic school traces its history back to the time of the early explorers. Some are inclined to suppose that the first colonies and schools were found in the English settlements of the New World. But the earliest settlements in what is now America were in parts of the country outside the thirteen English colonies; schools were planted there as well.

When the first Catholic explorers and immigrants came to the New World, they were accompanied by their own priests. These priests, aware of the hopes and needs of their people, and of their dreams for their children, established Churches and schools from the beginning. They founded them not only for their co-religionists, but also for the natives and for other young people in their areas. These first schools were, in part, very like the schools the explorers had known in their own homeland, and in part, were new realities, adjusted to fit a new, very unique situation. Catholic immigrants too had new dreams in a new land. They were both practical and full of vision. They wanted to teach the young people in a new world to read, write, do simple arithmetic, to develop skills that would help them survive, and also to have a vision that would give them energy and hope to accomplish the great things that needed to be done.

The first Catholic school in the thirteen colonies was established by the Jesuits in Maryland in 1640, a hundred and thirty-six years before the founding of the Republic.[1]

Introduction

Since earliest days, Catholic schools have had a continuous existence in America. Some of the other denominational parochial schools also continue to the present, but their number has been greatly reduced, and many have now totally disappeared. Despite the fluctuations in the populations of these schools, it seems rather clear that the parochial school, in one form or another, will continue to exist here together with American public education. Even though only a modest percentage of the total population attend parochial schools, they will continue as long as freedom of religion continues to be important and possible in this country.

Parochial and public schools were both major factors in the development and in the continuance of American education. By state choice and the decision of the Supreme Court, most students will be educated at public schools. Whatever America is now or becomes in the future will, to a great extent, be determined by its educational program, especially by its public schools.

EDUCATION AND AMERICAN CULTURE

America has its own culture, shaped by its people and all its experiences. In turn this culture affects the way American perceive and judge all things. A culture is a complex reality. The culture of a great country has certain dominant features and tendencies: the great hopes and convictions of a people will affect its culture in many concrete ways. But the limitations and the flaws that affect the leaders and shapers of a society will in complex ways affect the cultural pattern as well. In a great nation there will be also a variety of subcultures. A culture does not simply happen; and it is not fixed permanently when it begins to take shape. Largely it is a product of many free choices of people who gradually shape their culture, and it can be altered by the free choices and the creative energies of those who find a culture flawed in certain ways, and in need of becoming a more human, better, and richer one.

Kroeber and Kluckhohn, in their well known study of culture, noted that before they began their book they surveyed and analyzed more than 160 definitions of culture. They then articulated their own extremely complex definition of culture.[2]

Culture refers primarily to the broad pattern that makes up a distinctive way of human living, for individuals and for the community. A culture deeply affects the way those who live in that culture perceive and judge and act, and it is affected by all that the culture experiences. The influence of culture does not remove freedom. Though the dominant tone of a culture might incline people to think in relativistic ways, or to engage in racist talk and behavior, people living in cultures are not simply driven by them to act and think in certain ways, but are in varying measures inclined to act in ways favored by the persuasive weight of cultural forces.

The Vatican Council[3] says of the importance of culture: "...man can come to authentic and full humanity only through culture, that is, through the cultivation of both natural goods and values. Wherever human life is involved, therefore, nature and culture are quite intimately connected." The infinite variety of ways in which the aspirations of a people might be shaped are helped to draw toward suitable and manageable directions by the many ways in which the reality of a culture inclines people. This led the Council to suggest the following account of what culture is. Culture involves many things:

"The word 'culture' in its general sense indicates all those factors by which man refines and unfolds his manifold spiritual and bodily qualities. It means his effort to bring the world itself under his control by his knowledge and labor. It includes the fact that by improving institutions and customs he renders social life more human both in the family and in the civic community." Finally, the Council states: "…it is a feature of culture that throughout the course of time man expresses, communicates, conserves in his works, great spiritual experiences and desires, so that these may be of advantage to many, even of the whole human family."[4]

Thus, the founding of the first American schools was the shaping of a cultural reality of the highest importance. The most profound experiences of those who came to a new world, amid many dangers, to find and pass on a better life to their children, led them to build schools of a spirit and a kind that could serve the future of those they loved. Schools would deeply affect everything, and be a chief instrument in the handing on of a culture and its hopes. But shaping schools does not fix them forever; and the hopes for schools becoming more effective over the years in every way for handing on the most important dreams of a culture must face all the forces in a culture — those we would reasonably judge best, and those we would reasonably judge mistaken. Those who love a culture must care that they help all in the culture shape the future of the culture in wise ways.

Culture, therefore, both shapes and is shaped by our way of life. It is itself man made, while it tends to make us what we become. The Council observes that "…men and women are themselves the artisans, the authors of the culture of their own community."[5] The wisest and most generous efforts to shape their world, aided also by grace, and the most foolish and selfish strivings of people, battle in the shaping of a culture. Every person, because he has a duty to help build a better world, has the duty to work with his fellow citizens to enrich and ennoble the culture of his people.

What a people expects of education will deeply affect a culture, as the educational institutions a people builds will shape their future. Today one must be aware of the sometimes excessive emphasis placed on certain areas of learning, such as science and technology. To be sure, these are certainly important areas of interest. But when cultural leaders shape schools in too narrow a way, and the schools shape too narrow a people, the whole culture suffers. Areas of study that reveal the special dignity and importance of man, and the realism of the highest human hopes are severely wounded when the area of stress in schools becomes too narrow. The Council warns that science and technology are not "…the supreme rule for discovering the whole truth." Unfortunately some confide too much in these areas and never "…penetrate to the intimate meaning of things." Mankind can be led to lose interest in transcendent realities and to despair of obtaining good things that the heart desires but material reality cannot confer.[6]

A richer culture enlarges the human spirit. It stimulates "a growth in the human spirit, ability to wonder, to understand, to contemplate, to make personal judgments, and to develop their religious, moral and social sense."[7] But this is not possible if the interests of students are pressed into too narrow a mold.

Because education is an important factor in the designing of culture, American schools will always be central shapers of American culture. A culture is indeed enriched by a National Museum, the Smithsonian Institute, and other extraordinary institutions. But nothing gives a better insight into the culture of the nation than the nature and quality of its schools and the way of life which they inspire.

The Supreme Court is another institution which must be examined. In interpreting the Constitution, the Supreme Court in a clear way defines the direction of both American culture and education. For example, Justice Brennan gives a restrictive understanding of education, believing it to consist of secular skills and aptitudes which can be effectively taught in public as well as parochial setting. He wrote these words in Lemon vs Kurtzman regarding Pierce vs Society of Sisters (1925) and Allen (1968) concerning the meaning of these important cases: "I read them as supporting the proposition that as an identifiable set of skills and an identifiable quantum of knowledge, secular education may be effectively provided either in the religious context of parochial schools or outside the context of religion in public schools."[8]

These pages will challenge the position expressed by Justice Brennan and maintained by far too many Americans.

What then has been the effect of education to this point in our national history on the American culture or the American way of life?

Justice Brennan answered part of the question. The part of the question left unanswered is: what effect will these two very different forms of education have on the American culture or way of life? What will religion and parental involvement versus their exclusion do in the teaching and learning of "an identifiable set of skills and an identifiable quantum of knowledge" on the way of life which Americans produce for themselves and for future Americans?

This brief study attempts to answer, in part, Justice Brennan's incomplete but illuminating statement. There may be insufficient data to judge the religious school's influence on American culture. There is, however, plenty of data on the role of the public school on American culture. Some judgment may be made about education without religion, without parental involvement, and with too great an emphasis on science and technology and their influence on the American way of life. We shall consider in this study this aspect of Brennan's incomplete statement.

The following pages try to recount how religion was removed from public education in America and how a secular philosophy of life has taken its place as the basis of that educational program. They likewise remind us that in these schools parents play but a minimal role beyond paying taxes. This study also seeks to point out how the Supreme Court of this nation confirmed those earlier educational decisions and made the official schools and institutions for our nation, as Leo Pfeffer states, not only secular and non-sectarian, but godless, thus defining so clearly both American education and culture.[9]

The question can now be placed: what culture results from this secular, parentless, and godless program which has become the official educational program in American culture in great part through the decisions of the Supreme Court?

NOTES

1) McClusky, Neil G., S.J., *Catholic Viewpoint on Education* (New York: Doubleday, 1959) 11; *New Catholic Encyclopedia*, Vol. 5, 1967, 169.

2) Kroeber, A. L., and Kluckhohn, C., *Culture: A Critical Review Of Concepts and Definitions* (New York, 1963 [reprint]), cited by *Catholic Encyclopedia* 4, 522 ff. Culture consists of patterns, explicit and implicit, of and for behavior acquired and transmitted by symbols constituting distinctive achievement of human groups, including their involvement in artifacts the essential core of culture consists of traditional (i.e.) historically derived and selected ideas and especially their attached values; culture systems may, on the one hand, be considered as products of actions, on the other as conditioning elements of further actions. 357.

3) *The Church Today: Documents of Vatican II;* ed. Walter M. Abbott, S.J., General Editor (New Century Publishers, Piscataway, New Jersey, 1966), 53

4) ibid., 53.

5) ibid., 55.

6) ibid., 57.

7) ibid., 59.

8) Lemon vs. Kurtzman, 89, 569, and 570, October 1970

9) Pfeffer, Leo, *Liberties of An American* (Boston, Beacon Press, 1956); cf. McCluskey, Neil, S.J.: *Catholic Viewpoint on Education* (Image Books, Doubleday, New York, 1962), 130.

Part I

Catholic Education in America

1. In the Beginning...to Pierce

2. Parental Responsibility and Catholic Education

3. Catholic Philosophy and the Curriculum

4. Catholic Education Leaders
   Monsignor George Johnson
   Sister Elizabeth Ann Seton
   Religious, Lay, and Pastors

CHAPTER 1

In the Beginning...to Pierce

To understand American Catholic education we must view it in relation to education in general, and specifically we must compare it with American public education. American public education is a special, indigenous creation. It has been developed by some fine minds and outstanding people into a unique force in the development of our individual and social life in this country.

Catholics boast of the educational programs established by the early missionaries as the first "schools" in this nation. Indeed they were; but they were very different from later American schools. Missionaries who accompanied the early explorers immediately established schools to teach the natives. Actually they transplanted their own homeland schools into the new world. Those schools had great value, but they do not compare with American schools as they exist today or even as they were conceived and structured over a hundred and seventy years ago. American schools are a new creation.

Jesuit scholar Neil McClusky points out that the first Catholic school in the colonies was established by the Jesuits in Maryland around 1640.[1] Probably the rightful predecessor of modern Catholic education was the Academy established by the Ursuline Nuns in New Orleans in 1727.[2] These early efforts marked the beginning of a long series of Catholic schools in this new world.

American schools in the public sector reach back to the time of Horace Mann, who in 1830 became the Secretary of the State Board of Education in Massachusetts.[3] The few trial public schools prior to that date were not successful. Catholic schools soon became a blend of the early Missionary Schools and the new American educational endeavors. Indeed the American influence became so marked that at one time Catholic schools had the reputation of being merely "public schools plus religion." That perception was strengthened by the many laws governing all American schools; Catholic schools were faithful to those laws. These factors did prolong the understanding that it was only religion added on to the public school curriculum that made a Catholic school. Changes in the Catholic school curriculum were made gradually, especially by immigrant teachers who presented translations of texts already in use in their native land. The total Catholicization of the schools, however, had to await the arrival of talented educators and certain gifted bishops who were dedicated to the idea of making education truly Catholic. Especially it awaited the work of Monsignor George Johnson, who was the American Catholic educator par excellence. He and his many students established what we know as American Catholic education today.

A generation after the birth of the nation and the American Revolution, in the early 1800's, very many sectarian schools were established in he United States. Each immigrant group, seeking religious freedom in the new world, established its own community which invariably included its own Church and usually its own school.

Horace Mann had a vision of a single, large public school system, educating all American children regardless of their religion. He believed that the religious schools in his day were dominated by the clergy and were strictly sectarian, that is, they were in the business of developing another group of children who would be members of the religious group sponsoring their school.

Although Mann's school would therefore be non-sectarian, not embracing any particular creed, the educator lived in an age in which religious education was considered a traditional and essential part of education, and he did not immediately interrupt that tradition. So along with the regular subjects in the curriculum he included his own version of Christian religious education.[4]

Mann believed that education was a function of the civil government. Since Church schools and private institutions did not provide for all the children, Mann's projected school would be the common school which would include everyone. (For a more detailed study of the role of Horace Mann, cf. Chapter 5 infra.)

Serious difficulties emerged with Mann's concept. Believing that education was important, that it should include religion, he nevertheless found general disagreement as to what should constitute such religious education in the common school. None disagreed with Mann on this point so much as did the Catholics.

While Mann and his followers were committed to Christianity, their commitment had significant limitations. They accepted only the Protestant version of Christianity. From the beginning, Catholicism was excluded from the public or Protestant school. Even Protestantism had to accept certain limitations. The Golden Rule, the Beatitudes, the Ten Commandments and certain moral and ethical religious teachings included in the Protestant Bible along with the Protestant principle of private interpretation, were considered sufficient to meet the public school's religion requirements. Consequently Mann allowed for Protestant teachings on some very important subjects: the inviolability of personal conscience, the right and sanctity of private judgment, without note or interpreter.[5] Many Protestant sects finally accepted Mann's version of religion as adequate for the public school.

The debate about this matter has been a long and difficult one, especially for Catholics. Mann was determined to exclude any sectarianism in the religion taught in the public schools, nor would he consider any compromises on this matter. As Neil McClusky put it: "A general Protestant, Christian influence should permeate the schools, but all specific sectarian influence was to be shut out."[6]

The bishops, speaking for the Catholic community, made it clear that Protestantism, even Mann's modified version of it, was not sufficient for the education of Catholic youth. The purpose of education, indeed the most important purpose, was to teach children the Catholic Faith as it is, and to rear them in a Catholic atmosphere. The conflict finally came down to one between Mann's concept of an appropriate version of religious eduation and the position of the Catholics.

Catholics wanted to provide their own program of religion for their own children and from the beginning they looked to the state for help in making this possible. The Catholic educational program now differs from that proposed by Horace Mann and his followers, but both the political and religious climate in those days, and even to the present time, has viciously militated against what seemed to Catholics to be a perfectly logical and reasonable request. An education based on Catholic as well as some American values was, after all, what the parents wanted for their children.

Before the 1800's, Catholic bishops initiated an effort to reach some sort of understanding with the existing civil government. This effort failed. The State of New Hampshire responded by forbidding tax funds to any denominational school. This occurred in 1792. Massachusetts followed with similar legislation in 1810. New York and Maine followed suit in 1820. In fact, this legislative process continued until such laws were passed in every state.[7] These same states did, however, continue the teaching of their own Protestant version of religion in the public schools.

Despite this unfortunate legislation the Church and her bishops continued to battle for a reasonable and acceptable solution to the religious education problem. Perhaps the best record of what happened from the early 1800's to the beginning of the twentieth century can be found in the proceedings of the various Baltimore Councils.[8] These were special meetings of the first bishops assigned to dioceses in the new nation. The first of these was held in Baltimore in 1820 and continued at frequent intervals until the famous Third Provincial Council of Baltimore in 1884.

At the first Provincial Council in 1820, almost all of the debate and discussion concerned education. Even at that early date the bishops stated that existing conditions required that Catholic schools be established. This concern about Catholic children attending public school and about the government making no provisions for the proper education of Catholic children was the main theme of the bishops throughout the nineteenth century. The Baltimore Council in 1884 echoed and summarized the principal concern of that era. Pastors were required, under the sanction of serious sin, to provide in every parish a Catholic school for parishioners. At least one-fourth of all legislation passed at that Council concerned education and its importance to the Catholic community.

In the 1840's the United States was besieged by a political movement which was clearly anti-Catholic, anti-Jewish, and anti-Negro.[9] The Know-Nothing Movement, a secret nativistic organization, held that anyone not born in America should go back to where they had come from.

It was this bigoted organization that protested then stole the marble stone presented for the Washington Monument by Pope Pius IX. This theft was carried out on March 6, 1854, and halted the construction of this important patriotic project for almost fifteen years.

At the very time that the Know-Nothings were most powerful, Catholic immigrants were flooding the country. About every ten years Catholic population doubled and, as McClusky points out, this tremendous increase would continue to the very end of the nineteenth century.[10]

At first, most of these Catholic immigrants came from Germany and Ireland. But by the end of the century, all countries of Europe were fairly represented. Immigrants came accompanied, sometimes, by their priests, and often by teaching sisters, who immediately set about establishing parishes for their flock. As a matter of fact, in a brief time, pastors had erected churches for their people as well as schools to educate their children. These schools became important in helping the youth as well as the adults adjust to the new culture and language in which they suddenly found themselves. They also benefited the nation by preparing immigrants, young and adult, for useful citizenship in their new homeland.

This tremendous growth in the Catholic population made the policies of the public schools even more rigid. Sectarian religious education was forbidden; Catholics were simply unwelcome. Catholics fought this policy. The larger the Catholic community became, the greater were the objections to Horace Mann's version of Protestantism. Anti-Catholicism seemed to increase in geometric proportions.

Catholics could not in conscience accept the truncated religion program formulated by Mann. Moreover, Catholics bitterly objected to the anti-Catholicism found in almost every area of the public school curriculum. The reading texts, even at the primary level, contained bigoted phrases and lessons. This was especially true of the history textbooks.[11] While Catholic educators were not influential in those days, the Catholic population was a mighty force that had to be reckoned with by the young and growing local governments of the United States. The bishops, whose responsibility it was to protect their flock, became outspoken critics of Horace Mann's educational program and particularly its anti-Catholicism and its modified Protestant religious education component. The bishops, not having any public forum available to present their responses and complaints, invented one. They established Catholic newspapers to bring their views on education and bigotry to public light.[12]

Bishop O'Connor of Pittsburgh, for example, wrote at length to the State Governor about the right which parents had to a religious education for their children. His diocesan newspaper carried his letter to the Governor:

"If a parent thinks the religious education of his child can be secured, or is best promoted, only in schools under ecclesiastical, or other control, which he respects, what right has the State to require him to act in opposition? Either that secular education is compatible with the religious education which he prefers, or it is not.

If it be, why not allow it to be gratified? If not, it is a grievance to press it. The man who values religion will not barter it, nor omit what will foster it, for any advantages that may be derived from mere secular education. To deprive him of all advantages of the public fund, because he will not receive it where he thinks he cannot lawfully do so, is to punish him for not violating what he believes to be his duty."

Bishop O'Connor clearly expressed his views concerning the place for the religious school in this country. He maintained that the public schools should be exposed to:

"…the salutary competition that would arise from other schools in which people have confidence, having a claim to a share of the public fund. By this they, too, will be stimulated to do well, and satisfy the public; reasonable demands will be complied with, and redress will be at hand when no other remedy is efficient. If the schools be as unexceptionable as their friends say they are, and admit they ought to be, no numerous class of people will forego their advantages. If their patronage would be diminished only when people think they can do better elsewhere, this should not be a ground of complaint."[13]

The school issue was in the early days the focal point of the unfortunate relationships between Catholics and other American citizens. Many saw in this issue an attempt on the part of Catholics to "take over" the state educational program. But it would be wrong to think that schools were the only issue. The situation was marked by remarkable level of bigotry and hatred which cut across every level of American life.

The Civil War (1861-1865) seemed at first to be a means to eradicate some of this hatred. Thousands of men were marching together on both sides of a terrible conflict. Catholics and Protestants were deeply involved and the courage and loyalty of all were openly tested. Catholic Sisters earned high praise for the service they gave as nurses during the war. The conflict, however, actually did little to overcome the problems of bigotry.

General Ulysses Grant, the great General of the North and later the President of the United States (1869-1877), betrays how difficult and deep was this problem. When addressing a gathering of Veterans during his presidential campaign, he publicly expressed his deep concern about "priestcraft", an obvious reference to the Catholic faith.[14]

In 1875 a new problem appeared on the horizon with the introduction of the Blaine Amendment.[15] A proposed amendment to the Federal Constitution forbade the federal government to devote directly or indirectly any money or land to schools having religious affiliation. Strangely enough, this proposal had its origin in that "priestcraft" campaign talk which General Grant gave to a group of Civil War Veterans. Blaine was hoping to win the favor of the president by his action. The popularity of such thinking is illustrated by the fact that eleven such proposals were made at the federal level.

James Gillespie Blaine had an interesting background for the work he did in putting Grant's proposal together. His Catholic cousin, Ellen Ewing Sherman, was the wife of General William Sherman; and Mother Angela Gillespie, CSC, was a cousin as well as the American foundress of her religious order. Blaine himself was a baptized Catholic, and may have even received some instruction before he lapsed from Catholicism. He carefully concealed certain facts about his life, especially how his father was a convert on his deathbed and was buried in a Catholic cemetery. Publicly Blaine claimed to have affiliation with several Protestant groups, especially Presbyterians and Congregationalists.

The Amendment proposed by Blaine was a serious danger for the Catholic community. When the Federal Constitution was formulated in 1789, it contained no reference to education. This was the main bargain made by the federal government with States. Education would be in the sole province of the States and, beginning with New England, each state moved in and took over its role in education. It was in the New England area that Horace Mann got his start. The first law denying any tax help to religious schools was passed by the State of New Hampshire. Early in our history, Catholics recognized that any hope for Catholic education must come from the federal level. Now the Blaine Amendment threatened any possible federal help. Fortunately, the Amendment and its clones were not approved, but it did give a clear indication of the hopes and aims of many citizens, and especially of some political leaders who wanted to please them.

The complaints of the Catholic bishops were clear, unmistakable, and legitimate. Before the Civil War, McClusky tells us that least ten states had attempted to continue both Catholic and public education. He goes on to note that "…at one time or another in our national history nearly every state in the Union has had some such (cooperative educational) plan in operation."[16] He points to the most notable compromises in the last century: the Poughkeepsie, New York, and the Farribault, Minnesota compromises. These plans involved the Public School Board's leasing a Catholic school building, and paying the maintenance and operation costs, including teachers' salaries. The pastor arranged religion classes before and after school hours. Although less than ideal arrangements for the Catholic community, they were important compromises. Especially did they demonstrate that arrangements were possible if both sides would cooperate.

In the meantime, bishops moved ahead with local plans. Where the atmosphere was good, some reasonable solution was achieved with local government and school authorities; where the atmosphere was clouded by bigotry, such special arrangements could not be made.

Bishop John Hughes of New York submitted a recommendation of great symbolic as well as practical importance. The incoming Catholic community once began by building a church for worship by their congregation. Bishop Hughes now proposed that a school be erected first. This accelerated the growth of Catholic schools and demonstrated clearly the importance which the Church and the Catholic people placed on education.

Bishop John Lancaster Spalding took the lead in the third Plenary Council of Baltimore (1884). As noted, the school issue was so important that the major part of all the legislation passed by that Council concerned Catholic schools. It was in that Provincial Council that this famous legislation proposed by Bishop Spalding was approved: "Near each Church, where it does not exist, a parochial school is to be erected in two years…and is to be maintained in perpetuum…all Catholic parents are bound to send their children to the parochial school."[17] Certainly this was an extreme measure, but the extent of the anti-Catholic bigotry, both within the school community and outside it, was almost beyond belief.

The bigotry so evident at the beginning of the nineteenth century continued throughout the century. One Catholic response to the terrible wave of bigotry against "Popery" and the hatred of Catholic schools was an abundance of writings from bishops. This came both in the form of decrees by Councils, local and Provincial, and by their personal writings. The Catholic newspaper was probably the first public forum used by the bishops. As already noted, Bishop Michael O'Connor had established the Catholic newspaper shortly after he became Ordinary of the Diocese of Pittsburgh in 1843, and he used it as a platform to express himself freely and completely on the school issue and other relevant matters that affected his diocese.[18] There are numerous examples of such efforts made by other bishops.

Of particular interest was the organization of the Knights of Columbus by Father Michael J. McGivney[19], the Assistant Pastor at St. Mary's Parish in New Haven, Connecticut. In 1882, this new organization was chartered by the State of Connecticut. Today it can be found in every state of the Union.

The Knights of Columbus has a two-fold purpose: dedication and loyalty to the Church; service and loyalty to the nation. The Knights of Columbus were well aware that it was the general opinion of bigoted Americans that one could not be a good Catholic and serve the church, and at the same time, be a good American and loyal to the country. This assumption the Knights set out to uproot.

For over one hundred years the Knights of Columbus have distinguished themselves by witnessing both their love of God and His Church and their loyalty to their country. Because in many ways the Knights of Columbus expressed by their very existence precisely what the nineteenth century problem was between the Catholic faithful and many citizens and civil authorities of the country, the organization's record expressed clearly the Catholic community's answer to this terrible bigotry and indicated that Catholics stood firm on their allegiance to their church and to their country.

The turn of the century, a period of tremendous immigration during which Catholics from every country in Europe made their way to the United States, marked a time of special significance. Bringing families and children, and often their priests and sisters, Catholic immigrants established themselves quickly in places where they could find work in the many mills and factories appearing throughout the states since the Industrial Revolution.

In the year 1900, the Catholic population in the United States doubles[20], reaching over ten million. Like other immigrants, Catholics were looking for simple yet important things: a job, a home, their own church, and an education of their choice for their children, the freedom, justice, and respect for humanity America had promised. But the anti-Catholic forces, who had taken over the country and had threatened its promised way of life, resented these "intruders," especially in the continuing conflict between public and Catholic education.

Within a few years, especially as a result of the Baltimore Council, Catholics had erected numerous schools and churches, established rectories for their priests, convents for their teaching nuns, and had enrolled 854,523 children in school.

Shortly after the turn of the century, it was clear that the world was heading for another armed conflict. While amazing things were occurring on the home front (the invention of the automobile, airplane, telephone — and so many other things), the international scene presented a gloomy picture. With the assassination in 1914 of the Archduke, heir to the throne of Austria-Hungary, came reactions leading to the greatest war to that point in our history — World War I.

Never before were so many people — women, children, and soldiers — killed in a war; never were so many nations involved. Some nations were completely obliterated; millions of people were killed. The United States became a part of the horrible conflict on April 2, 1917.

Of the ten million young men who volunteered, a million-man army was selected. Fifty-two thousand soldiers were killed. On November 11, 1918, the disastrous war ended.

The victory was a great one in our history and was properly celebrated as a historic event by all the people.

In the light of such world turmoil, the bigotry, conflict, and hatred over Catholicism in America seems insignificant. Did not everyone — Catholic, Negro, Jew, Protestant — come to the aid of their country? Did not the cooperation demonstrated make us the most powerful nation at war? Certainly, if we can come together at war, we can do the same in peace.

With the cheers and excitement still ringing in the ears of the happy citizens, certain forces active in the State of Oregon decided to bring its religious conflict of hate to a head. Using the plea of democratic unity and maintaining that Catholic schools were divisive, in Pierce vs. Society of Sisters it was argued that all children should be compelled to attend public schools. This famous case, based on the Compulsory Education Laws and geared to destroy once and for all the Catholic educational system, finally made its way to the Supreme Court.[21] On June 1, 1925, the Court declared unanimously that the 1922 Law proposed by the Scottish Rite Masons and aided by anti-Catholic bigotry, especially inspired by the Ku Klux Klan, was unconstitutional.

Justice McReynolds delivered the Court's decision: "The child is not the mere creature of the States. Those who nurture him and direct his destiny have the right, coupled with the high duty, to recognize him and prepare him for additional obligations."

After being in the school business since the time of the explorers, and continuing through the founding of the new republic; after living through hatred and bigotry from the beginning of the eighteenth century and throughout the nineteenth century; the highest court in the land acknowledged the right of parents to provide schools of their own choice for their own children. What a tremendous victory for Catholics and all parents who wanted to educate their children as they saw fit! They not only have the right, said the Supreme Court, they also have the "high duty" to educate their children as they wanted to.

Not only religiously concerned parents rejoiced but also those who philosophically maintained that the state is not the educator and should not supplant parents in this important role. They, too, rejoiced in the Oregon State decision which clearly acknowledged parental rights in education.

The entire country enjoyed the victory of the 1925 decision by which parents could legally establish their own schools for their own children and teach their own values, ideals, and religion. Their life and beliefs constituted no threat to this great Republic.

This historic decision on the essence of our human and social life is in harmony with the principles of Catholic philosophy. As Jacques Maritain observed:

"...For just as man is constituted a person, made for God and for a life superior to time, before being constituted a part of the political community, so too man is constituted a part of family society before being constituted a part of political society. The end for which the family exists is to produce and bring up human persons and prepare them to fulfill their total destiny. And if the State too has an educative function, if education is not outside its sphere, this function is to help the family to fulfill its mission, and to complement this mission, not to efface in the child his vocation as a human person and replace it by that of a living tool and material for the State."[22]

Maritain, in this one paragraph, explains clearly the proper role of all the actors on the stage of life.

NOTES

1) McClusky, op. cit., 11

2) *New Catholic Encyclopedia,* Vol. 5 1967 – Education, 129

3) McCluskey 7; Dunn, William K., *What Happened to Religious Education* (John Hopkins Press, Baltimore, 1958), chap. 2

4) ibid., 9 ff.; cf. Dunn, 125, 134, 137

5) ibid., 9; Dunn. 135, 137

6) ibid., 10, cf. Chapter III; Dunn, 138

7) O'Neill, J. M., *Religion and Education Under the Constitution* (New York: Harper Bros., 1949), 141 ff.

8) *New Catholic Encyclopedia,* Vol. 2, 38 ff, Szarnicki, Henry A., *Michael O'Connor* (Pittsburgh: Wolfson, 1975) Chapter 7, 24; cf. McClusky, 16 ff.

10) McClusky, 21

11) ibid., 11, footnote; cf. Dunn, 208 ff.

12) Szarnicki, 49 ff.

13) ibid., 130, 133, Letter to Governor, Commonwealth Journal (letter cited in Pittsburgh Catholic)

14) *Catholic Encyclopedia,* Vol. 2, Blaine, 598

15) ibid, 587

16) McClusky, 18

17) *Catholic Encyclopedia,* Vol. 2, 38-43; cf. McClusky; 17, ff,

18) Szarnicki, 49 ff.

19) *Catholic Encyclopedia,* Vol. 8, 215

20) McClusky, 21, ff

21) Pierce v. Society of Sisters, 268, U S. 510, (1925)

22) Maritain, Jacques, *The Rights of Man and Natural Law* (Doris C. Anson, trans.) (New York: Charles Scribner, 1943), 78, 79

CHAPTER 2

Parental Responsibility and Catholic Education

From the days of the explorers to the present time bigotry and prejudice expressed in the form of hatred of the Catholic Church and its schools continued to harass citizens of the new world. What is it that is so frightening about the Catholic Church and causes people to make such negative responses to it? And why is this public venom manifested so fiercely and consistently toward the Catholic schools?

As we consider these questions, we recall some of the reasons given for this bigotry. Horace Mann, for example, openly hated the Catholic Church and schools because he believed that "the Pope forgives sins in return for payment of money and grants permission for further sin if more money is forthcoming." He also spoke of the Pope as "that Vice Gerent of Hell, the Pope of Rome."[1]

Because education was so vital to the success of the new nation, some were convinced that the Catholics were eagerly seeking to take over all the schools.

Many could not understand why Catholics held so fast to their official teachings; why did they insist on Catholic nuns teaching religion to their own children and therefore undertake the costly maintenance and operation of schools for educational purposes? These and many other suspicions alienated the majority of citizens from Catholics in the new land.

Certainly Catholics have made many mistakes, Divine in origin, the Church has been very honest about the fact that their hierarchy and members are merely human and therefore subject to all the weaknesses of human nature. Some mistakes were made. Even today Catholic schools are far from perfect, yet they are the result of unspeakable and immeasurable sacrifices made by the Church and its members. They are also the source of great hope in the Catholic community. Nevertheless these schools continue to be a direct target of those opposed to parochial schools. Especially those in the American educational establishment, including certain scholars, textbooks suppliers, administrators, teachers, their unions, as well as ordinary anti-Catholic constituencies who deride Catholic schools as "divisive," especially in a democracy where the proper way to educate children, they maintain, is to keep them together.

Some say that the harshest enemies of the Catholic Church are those who have abandoned her. Others hold that no one leaves the Church because of something they cannot accept but because of something they cannot have. Countless scholars and students of society and religion have tried to discern why anti-Catholicism is so common and often so vehement. In the earliest days of our country, the burning of convents, rectories, churches and schools was a common event in most of our cities. Anti-Catholicism stems from such philosophical principles as pragmatism, scientism, secularism, hedonism, and instrumentalism which attempt to denigrate the teachings of Christianity. The well-being or happiness promised by these philosophies are self-defeating because they center on the self rather than on the other.

These pages attempt to present a rational description of the principles of Catholic life and education in the hope that clearer understanding may reduce prejudice.

In order to form "the good citizen" or to achieve the social good, all public educators seem to agree that formal education must be confined to the consideration of the natural, material, and social orders. In public education there is no level which exceeds these; it can aspire no higher. Any consideration of another real level would "perpetuate garrulous absurdities."[2]

Catholic education, on the other hand, is based on the philosophy of life and a faith which involves the acceptance of a level clearly beyond the natural, material, and social, the supernatural level. Built upon the natural, the supernatural concerns God and the things of God. How does one learn about the supernatural? God reveals to humanity not all truths but those aspects of the total truth which people should know and act upon. To Catholics, it is inconceivable to ignore what God reveals.

As people of Faith, Catholics also trust the gift of reason which God grants in order for us to understand the world in which we live and its people. For Catholics there is no conflict between faith, or what God reveals, and reason, or what we can discover by our own efforts.

As Pope John II noted in his recent Encyclical on Faith and Reason, "…there is a profound and indissoluble unity between the knowledge of reason and the knowledge of faith."[3]

Catholics accept with both faith and reason that God is real and that the divine reality exceeds anything human beings can imagine. Everything begins with God. Since God is the creator of the universe, which includes humanity, all belong to God and are destined for God. Catholic Philosophy explains this by stating that God is both the efficient and the final cause of man. This basic fact is essential in understanding a basic principle of the Catholic Philosophy of life: God made us for Himself.

Catholics believe in the Trinity; that is, they believe that God is only One but at the same time there are three Divine Persons in God: the Father, the Son, and the Holy Spirit. The work of creation is attributed to God the Father; the Son took on human form and as God-Man dwelt among us and redeemed us. During this time He taught us the meaning and purpose of life died on a cross for the sins of humans, founded the Holy Catholic Church, rose from the dead to demonstrate His Divinity, and then returned to His Father in Heaven. The Holy Spirit, the third person of the Blessed Trinity, also sent by the Father, continues to this day to sanctify guide, and teach us through the same one, holy, apostolic, and Catholic Church.

In summary, then, we were not only created by God but we were also created for God. This union with God comes about through Jesus Christ Who redeemed us. The effects of this redemption continue to be available to those who willingly coop- erate with God's plan and who seek the assistance of the Holy Spirit through the Holy Catholic Church.

God wants humanity to be very much concerned with life in this world and the creatures who sojourn here. The principal Christian Law, according to Jesus, is that we are to love God and also love our neighbor.[4] The charge so often made that Catholicism is Platonic, or otherworldly, is false. Catholics believe that real life is with our neighbors and eventually with our God. This can be understood more clearly by examining a distinction which Catholic philosophers make at the very beginning of the discussion of goals.

First, note the distinction which Catholic philosophers make between the *ulti- mate goal* and the *immediate goal*. As these terms indicate, Catholic philosophy (and therefore Catholic education) maintains that human beings seek to be ultimately unit- ed with God eternally in knowledge and in love. This "perfect happiness" exceeds anything that can be described in words. The Bible puts it this way: this ultimate union, or as it is technically called, this beatific vision, is perfect union of an individ- ual with his God, and is something that "…eye has not seen and ear has not heard…what God has prepared for those who love Him."[5]

Sometimes this union with God is referred to as eternal life, perfect love, per- fect beatitude, or perfect happiness. This complete happiness is the object of every- one's search throughout life, but it will never be realized fully until it is attained final- ly through union with God.

Saint John tells us that God is love and that we His creatures are His children. When Jesus was asked what the greatest law for His children is He responded in this way: "You shall love the Lord your God with all your heart, with all your soul and with all your mind…you shall love your neighbor as yourself."

Love, therefore, is the very essence of our Christian life and of our relation- ships with God and neighbor. Without a doubt this is at times a difficult way of life, a struggle, especially when the criterion is to love others as one loves himself, a very difficult standard to observe. Catholics believe in original sin which has left us weak and with a propensity to sin or evil. Sin is real and it consists in doing our own self- ish desires rather than the things God expects us to do. Original sin darkens our mind and weakens our will so that we cannot always know the right thing to do and we do not always have the will to do what should be done. Catholics also believe that God can give and help them through His grace and guidance. This grace combines with our own nature and makes possible certain thoughts and actions which constitute a supernatural way of life for humans. The Laws which God gives us in various ways provide guidance in knowing what should be avoided and, on the other hand, what can be trusted during the challenging journey of this lifetime. Thus, we express our love of God and gain eternal happiness and love in union with God only when we cooperate with His Grace and guidance.[6]

Union with God, then, is our final Goal, which can be attained when we live the way God expects us to live in this life, that is, by loving God above all things and loving our neighbors as we love ourselves. This can be accomplished by accepting God's Grace and following His rules for this life.

The Church is deeply concerned with time and history. She actively promotes the values of a temporal common good. That good is subordinated to the final end of the human person, but it is a real good and therefore not only a means to eternal life. Man cannot ignore nor be indifferent to this life. On the contrary one must live it to the fullest and thus be guided through these temporal goods to the final end. Life as lived in this world is very real and very important. It is also the measure of our worthiness for the final end.

Fortunately, there is a model for all of us: Jesus Christ, true God and true Man, who lived among us to show us how we should accomplish this. He presents Himself as…the Way, the Truth, and the Life. It is in following Jesus, in imitating Him as well as we can, that the supernatural way of life can be lived and that wonderful union with God in eternal life (or eternal happiness) can be achieved.

The restoration of true happiness to the individual is through the establishment of union with God in this life in so far as this can be achieved or imperfectly now and forever perfectly in the next life.

This imperfect union necessitates the development of one's natural powers and the re-integration of these natural powers with the supernatural life of grace. It demands the re-creation of the image of God in us. It requires that one be led to seek by natural powers *truth, goodness,* and *beauty,* and be so directed in his search as to arrive ultimately at God, Who is eternal Truth, Goodness, and Beauty. It demands a conformation of one's personal and social acts to the rule of right reason as ordained by divine wisdom.[7] These immediate goals are achieved when teachers (and parents) seek to do the following:

SPECIFIC AIMS[8]

1) To develop the native abilities of the individual to their optimum levels.

2) To develop the individual in the likeness of Christ.

3) To supply experiences which will develop ideas, skills, habits, and attitudes necessary to meet the modern challenge of Christian living.

4) To prepare the child to meet this challenge in the environment of American democratic society.

5) To make available for the individual the cultural heritage of the race.

6) To help youth understand and cherish those basic life principles which are eternal and changeless so that such principles may become governors of conduct in the individual.

7) To develop in the individual the ability to adapt easily to change.

8) To clarify for the individual the relationship to God, the Church, other people, nature, and self.

MODIFIERS OF BEHAVIOR

To develop the general aim and the specific aims, each teacher in every class, and at every grade level, should plan to establish in the pupils modifiers or controls of conduct, which in Catholic terminology are called virtues. A virtue is a habit. It is a learned tendency to act always according to right reason or in conformity with the law of God. Virtue implies strength, activity, and joyfulness, and is something very positive, not negative. There is no such thing as a passive virtue. Human intellectual, volitional, and emotional abilities are all involved in the formation of virtues or good habits. A habit which directs an individual towards the ultimate goal is a virtue. A habit that leads one away from his final goal is a vice. The task is to build up virtues by cultivating them throughout life.

Virtues are either natural or supernatural, depending on whether they arise out of a natural or supernatural motive, and whether or not they are directed towards a natural or supernatural end. To be practical, one should develop the virtues on a natural level first, and then on a supernatural one. A natural virtue may be defined as a habit which exercises some native and God-given power of the soul, a power which belongs to us by nature. It is a power acquired by natural means from natural motives which directs one to a good natural end. When the end and the motive of the habit become supernatural we call it a supernatural virtue.

We regard these virtues as the specific controls of conduct which we attempt to develop in the lives of our pupils. Specifically these controls of conduct are the following:

CARDINAL VIRTUES: So called because on these main or "hinge" virtues depend a host of other virtues.

1) Prudence: The habit of controlled direction of human acts in accordance with right reason. It develops a certain perfection in choosing the proper means to an end. It demands rightness of action and ends that are good.

2) Justice: The habit of giving to all what pertains to them and of respecting the rights of others.

3) Temperance; The habitual conformity of sense appetite to reason, when these appetites prompt one to adopt a course contrary to right reason.

4) Fortitude: The habitual conformity of sense appetite to reason, when these appetites prompt one to give up some reasonable course of action.

SUPERNATURAL VIRTUES: God's gift to us that we may know and love Him as our goal in life. These are called Theological Virtues.

1) Faith: The virtue by which we believe in God and all He said and revealed to us., and all that the Holy Catholic Church proposes for our belief, because God is Truth Itself.

2) Hope: The virtue by which we desire eternal life as our happiness, placing our trust in God's promises and relying not on our own strength but on the help of the Grace of the Holy Spirit.

3) Love (Charity): The virtue by which we love God above all things for His own sake, and our neighbors as ourselves for the love of God.

The immediate aim of Catholic education, then, is the virtuous life, that is, to achieve union with God in so far as it can be accomplished in the time and circumstances in which we find ourselves. It is a union with God which can be achieved by a child, by a youth, by an adult; it is one that we can achieve at every stage of growth in our life. It is accomplished by recognizing and accepting God's revealed teachings, learning those truths, and developing those virtues which give growth to the individual and which come to him or her through the various educational agencies in our society and, of course, through the Grace of God.

In every age in Church history, moralists have grappled with the human situation to find ways in which they can enable the human community to realize the values embodied in the Ten Commandments, the great Commandment of Love, and a life characterized by the cardinal virtues of prudence, justice, temperance and fortitude and the theological virtues of faith, hope and charity. Moralists try to mediate the moral values of our religious tradition to people whose way of thinking and of acting have been deeply influenced by the culture in which they live.[9]

There are, to be sure, many educational agencies in society. But not all are dedicated to bringing God's word and Grace to us. The family the state, the church, and indeed society itself reflect a collage of ideas and images which may lead to God or at times may lead away from God. One can list countless other agencies in our society which affect the growth of the individual, positively or negatively, such as television, radio, the newspaper, theater, books, the home, and on and on. The one formal agency to which all segments of society look to for the education of its youth is *the school*. In the school, through planned and controlled experiences the children are guided toward the achievement of their immediate goals in this life and therefore its ultimate goal in the next life.

It must be noted clearly that the school, is not the only agency in education, nor is it necessarily the most important or influential, but in our culture the school plays an important and special role.

But even before the school, the special role of the parents constitutes the most important, the primary, and the most influential educational agency in the life of the child.

THE ROLE OF THE PARENTS

Our society rests on the pillar of the family. Because today some make enormous efforts to create substantial changes in the family, Catholic parents must have a clear concept of what is meant by the family in Catholic life and Catholic philosophy of education. Only thus can the family survive the attacks currently made upon it.

A Catholic family consists of a man and a woman, united in a sacred commitment and indissoluble bond of love and unity, and dedicated primarily to the generation, nourishment, and education of children. The family primarily seeks for all its members that virtuous life or immediate union with God which leads to the final and perfect union in Eternal Life. The act of generation or pro-creation is effected by loving intercourse between the man and the woman so united and so committed, and is, therefore, the most sacred and complete expression of their love. This act is such a powerful expression of their love and such a sacred and meaningful act that it is reserved to married couples exclusively. Through this act, loving couples, so united, consummate their holy bond and undertake the work given to them by generating with God's help new life. It should be noted clearly that sex does not equal love. Love, however, subsumes sex under the circumstances noted above. Sex is, in fact, an important component of this kind of bonded and committed love.

A mother and father thus united in such a sacred bond and who generate, nourish and nurture their children, thus demonstrate, from the beginning, that they have the sense of responsibility required for this state in life. Without this important sense, parenthood in all its beautiful aspects suffers, and so, too, do the children. Responsibility is the key to successful married life and parenthood.

The father, mother, and child (or children) constitute the family in the formal sense of the word. This has been recognized by the Supreme Court in the landmark Pierce Case: "The child is not the mere creature of the state, those who nurture him and direct his destiny have the right, coupled with the high duty, to recognize him and prepare him for additional obligations"[10] It is the duty of parents to conceive, to nourish, and to educate children. These parental responsibilities are so serious and so important that careful preparation for marriage is a necessary element in making this union successful. It is unfortunate but true that many people often can, and as a matter of fact do, enter marriage without the slightest awareness of its sacred meaning and its serious duties, privileges, and responsibilities. Before entering this sacred union, men and women must be properly prepared so that the children to the union are not simply conceived but are also properly nourished and educated.[11]

The education of their child which parents are responsible for begins immediately at conception. From that moment they must take special care to assure the child's proper development and growth by following appropriate nourishment habits and avoiding anything which could injure or affect adversely the growing unborn child.

Likewise, from the beginning parents are responsible for the education of their children by both word and example. Parents must do everything they can to encourage the child's physical, social, intellectual, and spiritual growth.[12] It is their special duty to demonstrate always, in word and example, the importance and sacredness of the holy bond that unites them as husband and wife, and as a family, and which is the root of the loving acceptance of the children God may send them.

In the earliest years of a child's life, parents are usually very careful about the growth of their children in physical, mental, and social ways. Unfortunately they are not always so concerned, especially in the first years of the child's life, about spiritual development. The Second Vatican Council reminds parents that the home is to be thought of as "The Domestic Church."[13]

It is the parents who make this a reality. The Church is God's house and this house serves to bring us before God to worship Him, to thank Him, to do penance and to pray for His help. Here Vatican II states that the home should also be considered as a church. In view of all the insights this and past generations have of the home this is indeed a revolutionary idea. It is not just a place to stop for rest, or to get nourishment, or to renew acquaintances with the family; the home is also a church and therefore should be a place sacred for many reasons, but especially because the family comes together there to be in touch with their God. It is in this sense that Vatican II reminds us that the home is the domestic church.

But if this is to be accomplished leadership is required. The church should be the first to encourage families to come together in their home as God's children. How often do they receive such encouragement? How often are their efforts in the home looked upon with suspicion? The church through her priests and other representatives must reach out and encourage this important way of living together.

Today there is a large movement toward home schooling, something which is received in a not too friendly fashion by many. Unfortunately, priests sometimes are very hostile to this effort. They especially must be helpful. Parents, they say, are the first, most important, and most influential teachers of their children – until parents attempt to do this.

What the church must do is offer to be helpful to such parents and through their representatives do everything possible to see that this worthy parental task is properly fulfilled.

Chapter 2 – Parental Responsibility and Catholic Education

The unique position of parents did not come into existence recently. On the contrary, the role of parents is inherent in the very nature of parenthood. As such, the parental role must be respected and honored.

As one looks back in his own family he may be fortunate enough to find this very form of education. In Chapter 11 of this work a very treasured story of my grandfather's involvement in this effort, almost a century ago, is recalled. He was noted in the family for his love of the family Bible and the frequent use of it to instruct his children and grandchildren. I am a living witness to that teaching event in my grandfather's life.

Parents and children need the help that only their parish priest can give. They must know that the church approves of their home teaching tasks and that the church is eager to help and guide them regarding such undertakings. An occasional homily on this topic does tremendous good. In this way parents learn that they are not alone in what can be a gigantic undertaking. Thus, families should pray together frequently and at meaningful times; they should go to church together as a family, taking their children with them as soon as reasonable; parents must be keenly aware of the need to be kind, good, and understanding to their family and friends, to their neighbors, to strangers, and especially to the needy. Parents must observe in appropriate ways Church feast days and holy days while involving the children to the degree possible. If Advent is simply a shopping season instead of a solemn preparation for the birth of Christ, parents have missed the point and so will the children. The secular aspects of Christmas and Easter should be celebrated in a reasonable fashion but the religious meanings must be given the primary place in the domestic Church. Showing in proper ways their deep love for one another will strengthen the marriage bond and thus the family. Perhaps the most important thing is to create an atmosphere of love and care in their home.

It has been said that many of the child's most important characteristics, such as its temperament, attitudes, likes and dislikes, are formed before the child darkens the doorway of any school. There was a saying (by whom I do not recall) that if one works diligently with a child from birth until it is ready for school, formation for life will be set. If this is true, so, too, is the opposite. Hence, mother and father together must seriously and collaboratively be zealous about the great trust that God has given them.

Oftentimes we think that this period in early childhood is simply a preparation for going to school. At most, that preparation is only a part of the total task. These few years could be the only years given the child. If such would happen, we can comfort ourselves with our philosophy of life and education which teaches that through baptism the infant is already prepared, even at an early stage, for eternal union with God.

Nevertheless careful preparation of the child for school is one of the important duties of parents. If possible, they should arrange to visit the school and meet the future teachers of their child. They should develop in the home an academic friendly atmosphere which will be authentic and congenial to learning. There should be good books, good magazines, decent pictures, and Catholic newspapers in the home, and the parents should take time to show personal interest in such important and admirable learning tools. Reading to youngsters is a definite help in their learning process. Their interest in learning will be reflected primarily in the example given their children who readily take up the habits of their parents for good or for evil.

Before me now is the famous family Bible which grandfather used. It is dated 1865 and it is noted "...from the last London and Dublin editions, carefully printed from the edition of 1844 which was published with the approbation of the Most Reverend John Hughes, D.D., Archbishop of New York." That 4.5 x 10 x 13≤ volume was a constant companion of my grandfather and it was not just a symbol. He used it to learn and to teach and, as far as possible, to make his little home church-like. The volume is about the same age as my grandfather, since he was born, according to our best records, in 1865.

From the moment this volume came into his possession until the present moment it has never been out of the family. From grandfather it was passed along to my father, the oldest son, and when my parents died it went along to a cousin who preferred that it come to me. It now has a privileged place in my library.

My parents did their very best to carry on that teaching mission of their state in life. As a child I can remember sitting with my mother on the front porch and listening to her read from the family Bible — it was a precious time in our life.

While both parents felt obliged to read and teach, they did it in a vastly different way. My father was very conscious of his obligation to carry on this work and he did it like a soldier. We knew that it was something very special that was taking place. His sessions were very rigid.

My mother's sessions were more relaxed. She read to us and taught us just as she prayed. While my father knelt straight as an arrow while praying, my mother relaxed. Somehow that approach was a little easier on everyone. Just as she sat on her chair and fingered her beads in the afternoon, so too did we all relax and listen to her read the Bible to us. What blessed days they were.

As best as I remember I was in the first grade when I spied my mother in the kitchen fixing the Sunday roast. To my utter amazement she put the roast in the oven and then made the sign of the cross over it before closing the oven door. From that moment on she had a helper. I regularly blessed the roast with her, and the home-made bread, and yes, even our little puppy dog. My mother never said anything to me about this new duty and I never breathed a word about it.

My mother had her special way of praying and teachings. There was no pressure. Mostly you did what she did.

The early childhood period is also a time of preparation for going to church. There must be a significant and positive religious education input if early education is to be complete. A childhood, for example, without the Bible is certainly a waste of extraordinary opportunities to teach religious values. Many people have warm memories of lessons that they received from their own parents who were reading to them from the family Bible. Such wonderful opportunities should not be neglected. The love and respect which parents show through the use of important religious instruments and symbols are inestimable.

Just as the child is prepared for school, so too one must be prepared for church, As the parents would take their children to meet their future teachers in school and to examine with them all the great secrets in the schoolhouse that will soon become realities in the child's life, so too should parents introduce them to the "mysteries" of their parish church. This will happen not only through their own example, but by careful instruction in little things that soon will become so important to them. An afternoon's walk to the church for a visit, pointing out the many unique and wonderful secrets in the church, is every bit as important as a visit to their future schoolhouse. At that time they could be given the example of pausing for a moment to pray to Jesus hidden in the Tabernacle, and the parents can show by their own actions what it means to genuflect, to use holy water, to bless themselves, and where it is that one day, in the near future, they too will go to confession.

Indeed, the home is the "domestic church." Here they should be introduced into some of the future mysteries in which they will soon play such a crucial and critical role.

Although television, radio, and movies are powerful educational tools, they must be carefully monitored. Far too many children become victims of the overwhelming attractiveness of the media. Some children live in a world where they are exposed to television all the day long. This can have disastrous consequences. On the other hand, some parents have adopted strict rules about television, insisting that it not be allowed in their home. In one way this can be a great blessing for a growing child; but it also has its difficulties. Children will find it difficult in these times to live in a world without being exposed to television, and therefore it might be better if parents help them learn to understand TV's proper and controlled use during those important formative years. There can be little doubt that parents play the major role in educating the children whom they brought into this world. Their dealings with their own children must sometimes be very delicate and should always be thoughtfully planned if they are to be effective.

Parents should also take time to give their children some practical lessons in good citizenship. Planned discussion about voting, community activity and such other appropriate topics can give youngsters a good start on gaining a Christian attitude toward social living. Practical lessons on democratic living can also be developed in one's own home. Sharing responsibility and privileges constitute an important way for youngsters to understand and grow in Christian social living. Patriotism, by the way, is a part of the Christian virtue of piety. Good parents will strive to teach this important habit to their children. Family observance of important civic holidays gives ample opportunity to develop in youngsters this important quality of patriotism. My parents made it a practice to have the family attend every local parade possible. We all tried to participate.

Some parents must turn to child-care programs in order to assure the survival of their families. It is said that about 60% of our children are reared in a single parent family. These parents have special problems and need special help. Some parents, however, turn to child-care programs simply because they are too busy, or unfortunately, do not have the "taste" for family life that real mothers and fathers should foster. While there has been no final word on the success or failure of child-care programs, it seems to this writer that many children are in child-care, not because they must be, but because parents find it more convenient. Some children are hauled off to child-care centers at the break of dawn, and their parents bring them home in time for bed. The idea of family life developed is a sleepy "good morning", a goodnight kiss, and a nice warm crib. Such children never have an opportunity to learn very much about their parents, much less about family life. Besides the powerful lessons good family life provides, they miss the love which comes only from a caring mother and father.

Parents can give the child a proper start in life or they can set the child on the way to a troubled existence. Child care is not the normal way to help a child grow assured that life at home is truly secure, happy, loving, and worthwhile. Limited child care experiences may help but nothing can replace a good, positive family life. Family life can be wonderful and one of life's greatest experiences if parents take the time to make it so.

The child's home and family during these earliest years are the first church, the first school, and they are the first teachers in life. Those experiences, if satisfying, can mean much to the success of the formal education which follows.

If it is not a good and happy experience it could be the beginning of endless problems. Those early years are the time when lifelong impressions are made on young hearts and minds. Those early years are a time when certain realities in life make a deep impression: love; respect for others, other races and religions; having fun in the proper way; prayer; family life; fatherhood; motherhood; church; God; education in general, and so many other essentials which can make a deep impression, oftentimes lasting, on precious young minds.

Although many children, when they come to school for the first time, are able to sing the most complicated songs and do the most difficult modern dances, they are often sadly ignorant of how to bless themselves or say a simple prayer. Such poor home training could spell trouble in later years. Many of these problems are the consequence of young people rushing into the holy state of matrimony with little time for preparation, planning, or discussing possible problems; with little or no consideration of the spiritual meaning of what they are about to undertake. No wonder that so many marriages are quickly broken and so many children, the real victims of such broken unions, are on their way to an unhappy and difficult life, These children often perpetuate the way of life which their ill-prepared parents passed on to them.

As Dr. Cornelius Murphy puts it:

> Modern parents do not usually provide academic instruction; if they think of themselves as educators at all, they usually consider their role to be that of supporting the instruction that the child receives at school. Such support is valuable and, in some respects, indispensable. But parents can also unwillingly reinforce prevailing ideas concerning the purposes of education which are detrimental to the deepest needs of their children.
>
> When parents uncritically submit to the convention that the purpose of education is to facilitate employment and practical success. they collaborate in a social process which places their children in a servile position within a materialistic culture...if they take their calling seriously, they will avoid training their children to be subservient to the laws of the marketplace. It is part of the special dignity of parenting to make the family a school for love. Mothers and fathers teach by example, and they can show their children the integrity and fulfillment that can be theirs through a developing respect for truth, goodness, and beauty in all their inexhaustible wonder and diversity. In transmitting these values to their children, parents have the power to surpass the often-pretentious standards of modern pedagogy.[14]

The educational duties of the parents do not end when they take the child to school and to church. Parents continue throughout the life of their children to be the important teachers. Parents must be available to talk to their children about school problems and school life; they should make time in their daily schedule to help their children in a proper way with homework; and they should be available to help with the continuing problems of growing up. Parents must be available to help youngsters as they approach the difficult period of puberty and adolescence and they must be close enough to encourage them to talk freely about delicate matters which parents are expected to discuss with their children, especially in the area of sex. Parents must stand by during the difficult adolescent years and especially watch over their children as they begin to make their way from the family nest to a home of their own.

Their duties as religious educators will also continue throughout life. Parents must always be eager to explain church matters that may be a problem to a child. Children must know who their pastor is and why he is called the pastor. Likewise, if there are other priests around, the child must learn how to greet them, to listen to what they have to say. Just as religious enhance the church's life so will the presence of sisters and other church personnel be of interest to their children. They should be urged to talk freely to their pastor or priest and to seek counsel when it may be needed. Parents can teach very much to their children just by showing them how one should conduct themselves in the presence of others in the church family. Example is the great teacher, especially in religious and church matters.

The role of parents as educators continues even to the end of their life. By their example and words, through their prayers, their loyalty to God and the Church, parents show their children how marriage and parenthood can be successful and happy. Their example as parents and grandparents is another way of teaching their children how eventually to manage their own lives and homes when they make the decision to start their own families.

Finally, parents and grandparents can teach the greatest blessing of family life to their children, not only by the way they live, but by the way they accept the inevitable sufferings of life and finally death itself. What married life means, not only for those who are united in that holy bond, but for the children which flow from that union and grow up under the thoughtful eyes of dedicated and loving parents and grandparents, can be known only to God and to grateful children.

Barbara Bush has inspired audiences throughout the country in recent years through her lectures on "success." "Everything I needed to know to be successful I learned from my mother. Study, work hard, develop your talents, treat people fairly, trust in God. These are all the things my mother spoke about when I was growing up." We pray that we will have fathers and mothers who bring their growing children the same kind of sound messages, love, and happiness which that successful mother gave her daughter Barbara.

Catholic education indeed focuses on both worlds, the present and the eternal. Such education attempts to look at life as it really is. Our philosophy of life tells us that this world is not the be all and end all but there is for those who acknowledge the goodness of God's creation and who follow God's guidance and receive His Grace another world — one of total fulfillment... happiness and love.

Whatever analogy is used, it should be clear in the Catholic philosophy, life here and hereafter are most important for each person. From the brief picture given above it must be clear that a complete and full life in this world is a prerequisite for the life to come. The more complete, the more perfect, the more virtuous this life, the greater the promised eternal happiness and eternal union with God.

Catholic education spells out the specifics of this life for the one who has the heart aimed ultimately on the life to come. To achieve the immediate goal of Catholic education the students must strive for a life which is guided by the principles given on pages 15ff. One must strive to develop individual talents and abilities; live a Christian life by imitating Jesus and developing virtues; be ready to meet the challenge of a democratic society; seek out the cultural heritage of our race; develop basic life principles; be prepared to meet changes and make change; and understand our relationship to our fellowman, to nature, to self as well as to God and His Church

I commend to parents and other educators, the work of George Johnson, which develops these themes throughout.[15] This is the most positive response

Catholic education can make to the meaningless charge of total otherworldliness. The child developed on Johnson's concept of democratic life learns to experience the challenges of democratic life and its requirements, including free enterprise; economic democracy; the role of labor; importance of agriculture; private enterprise. Monsignor Johnson wrote long before the current flood of modern technology, but Catholic education is well aware and well prepared to develop children who must know and live amid recent technological developments. Dr. Johnson's approach to this will be examined in detail in the next chapter.

Christian social living develops youth in virtues which bring goodness to their life, family, and neighbors.

NOTES

1) Dunn, Kenneth K., *What Happened to Religious Education* (Johns Hopkins Press, Baltimore, 1958, 125.

2) James E, McClellan, "First Philosophy and Education," NSSE Yearbook (1981): chap. 11, 262.

3) "On the Relationship Between Faith and Reason," Pope John Paul II *(The Pope Speaks,* Vol. 44, 1) Chapter 2.

4) Mt. 22:37.

5) I Corinthians 2:9.

6) I Corinthians 13: 1-9; John 13,34.

7) Catechism of the Catholic Church, United States Catholic Conference 1994, cf. 1-25.

8) Quigley, T. J., McDowell, J. B., Handbook of School Policies and Practices, (Diocese of Pittsburgh [rev.] 1947, published for local use only), 1,22.

9) Catholic Encyclopedia, Vol, 16, 301.

10) Pierce v. Society of Sisters, 268, U.S. 510., (1925)

11) "Declaration on Education", Documents of Vatican II ed. Walter M. Abbott, S.J., trans. ed., Msgr. Joseph Gallagher, 3.

12) "Decree on the Apostolate of the Laity," Vatican II, 11.

13)"Constitution on the Church," Vatican II, chap. 2, 11.

14) Murphy, Cornelius F. Jr., Beyond Feminism: *Toward a Dialogue on Difference* (Washington, D.C., Catholic University Press, 1995), 160.

15) Johnson, George, Better Men for Better Times (Washington, D.C.: Catholic University Press, 1943).

CHAPTER 3

Catholic Philosophy and the Curriculum

The school is the formal agency for the education of children.[1] It is important to remember that although it may not be the most important nor the most influential agency in the life of children, for better or worse it has been selected to fill this privileged role in our society.

Since schools were first established in our nation, experiments about the structure of the school and debates about the school program have been undertaken. How long should a child attend school? When should a child begin school? What sort of division within the school would most benefit the youngsters? It should not be a surprise to anyone to learn that such discussions and debates still go on. Every level plan conceivable has been attempted throughout the school community, but a final, definite, and universal arrangement has not as yet been achieved.

Perhaps more surprising is that the school keeps expanding upward and downward. In recent years the thirteenth and fourteenth grades have been added on in the form of the very popular Community College. Over the years kindergarten has become a part of the elementary school. Since the success of "Head Start" in the sixties, this pre-kindergarten program has been widely accepted. Whether the relatively recent Day Care Program will win educational approval is difficult to say since it is not universally accepted. Other interests, not directly related to education, express concern about this new program and its educational value. Many so-called educators, on the other hand, think that education cannot begin too early and, in their judgment, the day will come when the new born baby will come directly from the hospital to a Child Care Center. There these youngsters can be given the best exercise, best meals, best medical care, the best educational program. It sounds strangely like the program sponsored by our socialist colleagues.

THE CURRICULUM

The curriculum is defined as all the experiences which the child has in school and which are planned by the school to achieve definite purposes.[2] In Catholic education these experiences must be planned to achieve special ends, namely, the immediate and the ultimate educational ends as stated in the Catholic philosophy of education. The

28

term curriculum includes four important elements in the educational process. Each is clearly responsible for making planned experiences in the school a reality and each must contribute toward a clear understanding of the Catholic purposes in education.

Children learn through exterior and interior stimulation. It is the teacher's responsibility to provide various stimuli to foster the child's individual development. They must seek to adapt the stimuli to the child's real native abilities and faculties. The degree to which educators successfully plan learning stimuli will determine to great measure how much learning the child will absorb.

These goals are referred to in Catholic philosophy as the *immediate* and the *ultimate* educational ends. The ultimate goal of Catholic education is eternal union in love and happiness with God in Heaven. The immediate goal is achieving this union of love and happiness in so far as it is possible at every level in this life. In the perfect sense Jesus Christ is the model. Through Him the ideals, the attitudes, habits or the virtues necessary for living like Christ in our American democratic society are developed. This is accomplished through the curriculum which is planned and developed by the school and includes four essential elements.[3]

(1) TEACHER TRAINING. Perhaps one of the most important elements of the curriculum is the proper training of the school staff. It is through the teacher that those experiences planned by the school flow to the students. Needless to say the teacher must be well grounded in the principles of Catholic life. Everyone, from the superintendent to the newest primary school teacher, must be taught to know and to live the principles of the Catholic philosophy of life and education. The teacher must reflect in his or her own life the inner convictions of the truth imparted. There are very few other agents more influential in the development of the child than the teacher. Teachers therefore must conduct themselves, both in and out of the classroom, in accord with the Christian ideals presented through the curriculum.

It is of tremendous importance that teacher training programs give the tools necessary to achieve this ideal in their own life as well as the skills of communicating these experiences to students. The teacher therefore must be well educated and must understand the ideal of Christian perfection. The teacher that fails in this regard cannot expect to communicate these truths to their students.

2) SOCIAL ACTIVITIES or what is often called co-curricular activities. This includes all activities that are common to a school: drama, athletics, assembly clubs, newspapers, forensics, language clubs, math and science associations, music, art, radio and television. These activities must be carefully planned and organized with the same care as the school course of studies. All these activities thoughtfully chosen serve to enrich the student's educational life and to give opportunities for further development in fields which could lead them to successful life careers.

These school activities or co-curricular activities must not be put together casually. They are also sources of learning and therefore they must be planned carefully and thoughtfully. Many schools find such programs not only a productive and enriching experience for students but they also serve to improve the instructional program by involving talented teachers as leaders in this learning process.

3) PROGRAM OF STUDIES. Although educators disagree on most subjects in education there is probably a consensus elementary among them on the program of studies, that is, on the list of subjects which should be taught at the elementary and secondary levels, or subjects for general education. With a few important exceptions Catholic educators would generally agree with that same list. That program of studies would look something like this:

Language Arts — Reading, Writing, Listening, Talking, Spelling, and Phonics. English (Grammar and Composition) and Literature at the more advanced level.

Fine Arts — Drawing, Painting, Poetry, Music, Drama, Dancing, Art.

Social Sciences — Geography, History, Civics, sometimes Problems of Democracy, or in Catholic schools, Christian Social Living.

Natural Sciences — General Science at the elementary levels; Biology, Chemistry, Physics, at the secondary level.

Mathematics — At both levels.

Health/Safety — At appropriate levels.

Physical Education — At both levels.

Vocational Arts — In varied doses depending on the needs of youngsters.

Computer Use — From the first grade.

Religion — The main addition Catholic Educational Philosophy makes to the program of studies. Religion includes Bible and Church Hisory.

4) COURSE OF STUDIES. It is the task of the Catholic school to present to the students at all times and in all ways the ideals of Christian perfection. Schools accomplish this through the curriculum and the curriculum includes, as noted above, four distinct elements: teacher training, social or co-curricular activities, the program of studies, and finally the course of studies. What has been carefully planted in the first three areas comes to fruition educationally in the course of studies. Here it is that the training of the teacher, the thoughtful organization of school activities, the list of subjects to be studied, come to fruition in the actual teaching program of the school. This outline breaks down the potential subject matter in each area. Actually this part of the program may be of greater concern to the teacher than to the students. It marks out the manner of teaching procedure in particular fields. These outlines must be based solidly on the Catholic philosophy in order to accomplish the objectives of Catholic life in education. Each subject must somehow instill the

Christian virtues just as surely as religion; justice and charity should permeate every subject, and God must be the core truth of all learning.

In presenting this major and most unique part of Catholic education the work of Monsignor Johnson in "Guiding Growth in Christian Social Living" will be followed.[4] His work represents a critical point in Catholic educational curricular development.

Johnson groups the daily experience of the young into five basic relationships.[5] These relationships serve as the means of distinguishing learning activities into as many distinct areas. It must be remembered that a single action can cut across several or all of these categories.

(1) THE CHILD'S RELATIONSHIP WITH HIMSELF. These activities consist mostly of the Language Arts and the Fine Arts. Thus, educationally, these include a long list of subjects: Reading, Writing, Speaking, Listening, Spelling and Phonics. These activities flow naturally into English (Grammar and Composition) and Literature.

This relationship also includes the Fine Arts: drawing, painting, art, poetry, music, drama, and dancing. The basic skills in this group of Language Arts and Fine Arts are intended to establish in a special way the child's self-idea, and develop solid self-esteem and self-confidence. Other learning can develop only if the self-image is good and sound. Unless the child has a good idea of self, the beginning and subsequent efforts will be weakened and often break down with further serious consequences. Nothing seems to accomplish this better than mastering the basic skills in the Language Arts and Fine Arts. To be able to read, write, speak or to make a drawing that merits hanging on the refrigerator door, helps develop that self-esteem and self-dignity so essential for learning. especially for beginners.

In Catholic education the development of this healthy self-image is aided by the fundamental religious ideas that each one is created in the likeness and image of God and that through Baptism the youngster is not only a creature of God but a child of God.

Students are also encouraged in these two areas to be on the look out for "the Truth" in the Language Arts and for "the Beauty" in the Fine Arts. This search which begins in such a modest way, has profound meaning later in life when they understand that God is *the good, the truth, and the beauty*. Thus they realize that God's Beauty and Truth (as also His Goodness) have traces in His creation and if we search carefully these can be found.

(2)THE CHILD'S RELATIONSHIP TO NEIGHBORS. All would agree that there must be room in the Curriculum for the Social Sciences. A youngster must learn that no one is alone in the world; no man is an island. Each one lives with other people; each lives in community. Each must have a real appreciation and genuine understanding that there are other people and other communities sharing this earth. The child must learn that others have a background, customs, records, individual and social traits, and traditions which differ from their own. This is important for a fuller appreciation and understanding of our neighbors. Children must be taught and helped to respect people of other races, other nationalities, other religions, and who practice other traditions: no man is an island; "Love one another as I have loved you." Therefore, the Social Sciences teach a number of important concepts. Through Geography one learns the location of the different people and different communities in the world and many things about the environment in which others live and how this affects their lives. Gradually one is able to locate all the different nations and different peoples in the world. Through History the distinct record of our own community and nation as well as that of other peoples and nations is known and appreciated. History familiarizes us with certain aspects of the varying backgrounds within which people live. The child cannot mature nor learn properly unless these things about ourselves and our neighbors throughout the world are understood.

Finally, the Social Sciences also include Civics, which is the study of how to live in community, especially in terms of existing institutions, local, national and international. Sometimes educators give this subject other labels, such as Problems of Democracy, but whatever name it is given, the aim is to familiarize students with those great institutions that embody the meaning and message and sometimes the operation of great national or international ideas so important to our way of life. Catholics present this latter content under the title of Christian Social Living and try to help the students understand something of their cultural inheritance and how the Catholic becomes a good Christian Citizen.

Religion helps us to understand that these "other" people are also children of God like ourselves and that they have problems as we do. They also were made in "the likeness and image" of God and must be respected, loved and lived with in peace. They, too, make mistakes like ourselves and desire to be forgiven. They are our brothers and sisters and they deserve our help, understanding, and affection.

(3) THE CHILD'S RELATIONSHIP WITH NATURE. Through these subjects the student learns about the physical world, both the animate and inanimate. General Science is a program which gives a view of the child's physical world at the elementary level and tries to develop a taste for further study of science. Biology is the study of living things and discusses the meaning of corporeal or physical life. Chemistry is a science that deals with the composition, structure, and properties of physical substances and the transformation they undergo. Physics is a science that deals with matter and energy and their interactions in various physical fields.

It is important to remember that although these Natural Sciences are important they are not the be-all and end-all of life. As students grow older they will discover many scientists and philosophers, both ancient and living, who have tried to find in these natural sciences the total explanation of life. The world is filled with naturalists who believe and teach that science in some form is the beginning and end of all things.

One cannot look around a room without realizing the reality of science in life. This is a technological age. Science, therefore, is extremely important for life. It does not, however, give an adequate or final answer to the questions: what is life? what is the purpose of life? where does life come from? what is life finally about? Good teachers will point out that sciences, even the most sophisticated, have many advantages but also definite limitations.

Religion makes a great contribution here by pointing out that in the world science depends on hundreds of specific laws. It is good to remember that these laws should be respected — they make the world go 'round. But it is also important to note that the great men and women whose names are so often associated with these laws did not "create" them. They merely discovered them and traced their proper use. A far greater power and intelligence created these laws for the benefit of all humankind.

The Mathematical Sciences are about numbers and number symbols. Through mathematics the student will learn some marvelous things. The learner discovers that there are certain relationships which can be quantified through mathematics, and in this way, often very complicated relationships can be better understood and explained. For example, the student discovers that light actually travels and that the speed of that movement can be measured. The same is true for sound. These measurements can be put into convenient formulae so as to give a more complete and understandable picture of some aspect of the universe in which we live. As will be pointed out later, these sciences are a rich source of understanding the goals which must be achieved in Catholic education.

Educators would agree that Health and Safety, not only for our own individual good, but for the benefit of society at large, and indeed the universe, should be included in the Program of Studies and therefore the Course of Studies. The survival of other communities and other nations, indeed, the whole world depends in many ways on each individual. The nuclear age has taught very much in this regard. Nuclear materials, in a very clear way, teach that world-wide effects are not uncommon. Certain diseases and behavior can often cause such widespread effects. Health and safety are not mere local and personal concerns. They can affect the entire universe. A good understanding of these facts can cause a deepening of our personal concept of self and a deeper love of God and our neighbor.

Most educators would agree that there should also be something in basic education about Vocational Training and certainly about Computer Science. Although these two subjects might be debated regarding their proper position in the educational world, nevertheless it seems clear that vocational training is necessary to some degree for one's own survival. St. John Bosco demonstrated this truth very vividly through his concern about the importance of vocational training of young men. Many young people simply cannot handle the science or even the ordinary academic curriculum. Many have aptitudes for vocation areas and should be given that opportunity. St. John Bosco reminded us that these students also need to know about their bonds with God, their neighbors and nature.

Computer science has become a valuable and important tool in today's world. Of course, that is exactly what it is. It is a tool, one of many that is available in this world, and it helps gather and understand more information and facts. Like other tools, over-use and dependence can create problems. Good teachers will be on guard for possible problems.

In preparing the Program of Studies, the list of subjects, almost general consensus is achieved. One subject which comes first on the Religious Educators' list and is absent from others is, of course, Religion.

RELIGION

(4-5) THE CHILD'S RELATIONSHIP TO GOD AND HIS CHURCH. Catholic educators accept the Program of Studies as listed above. Nevertheless, they also indicate that the Catholic Course of Studies is clearly different than the Public School Course of Studies. This is due to three essential matters which, in our philosophy of education, must be included if education is to be complete. The first of these is *religion*, which is the acknowledgement that we are creatures and therefore dependent on God.

Religion tells us that there are other things in life aside from nature, which is also a creation of God. All that is known about God and our relationship to Him is revealed to us by God or is the result of reason's study and analysis of these revelations as well as the world about us.

When we speak of a child's relationship to God we must note at the same time that there is also a clear relationship to God's Church. The revelations of God were made principally by the God-Man, Jesus Christ, Who is the Founder of the Church, and also the Son of God. Those revelations, so important to all, have been entrusted by Jesus Christ the Almighty God for safe keeping, and for teaching, to His One, Holy, Catholic and Apostolic Church. These revelations are to help us understand what life is all about and how God is our Creator, our Teacher, our Helper, our Guide, our Source, and our Final End. For these reasons we must listen to what God has to say through His Holy, Catholic Church, our Teacher and our Guide in this world.

The Church teaches us in many ways, but throughout the ages one practical way has been through an official Catechism. The most recent edition was updated in 1994 and was published shortly thereafter. The new Official Catholic Catechism divides the content of our relationship with God into four main parts: The Creed or teachings about our basic beliefs in God and in all that He has revealed to mankind, especially through His Son Jesus and His Church; the Sacraments instituted by Jesus for the moments of special grace available to us; the Commandments, which are God-given guides in our search for eternal life; and prayer, our communication with God, by which we express praise, thanksgiving, sorrow, and petitions to Him.

Chapter 3 – Catholic Philosophy and the Curriculum

Monsignor George Johnson, without a doubt the greatest Catholic educator of this century, wrote a book entitled *Better Men for Better Times*.[6] This extraordinary book explains the world from a Catholic viewpoint. Primarily he answered the question: Why Catholic Education in American Society? In 1943, Johnson began the writing of Christian Social Living, a three-volume work which presented Catholic education as it should be worked out in the Course of Studies for every subject and at every elementary grade level. This was his answer to the "how" of Catholic Education. Putting these two works together, the definition of Catholic education emerges brilliantly. This understanding of "Why and How Catholic Education?" is one of the main purposes of this present study.

Unfortunately, Monsignor George Johnson died before he could finish this work, but his directions, guidelines, and classes on the subject were so clear that his work was successfully completed by his collaborators and his talented successor and student, Monsignor Frederick Hochwalt. In this extraordinary three-volume treatise on Catholic education, Monsignor Johnson talks about the relationships which a person has and in which he must be educated. He does not artificially shorten the list of realities in this life. He proceeds grade by grade, subject by subject, to indicate under each heading the activities and learning experiences which the child should have if its goals are to be achieved. Johnson completed this important curricular work for the first through eighth grades before his death. It is a brilliant example of what Catholic Education should be.

As Catholic education fosters the child's growth in relationship to self, others, the world in which we live, in ways of dealing with the world, it focuses on the most important relationship in life, the child's relationship to God and His Church. It is essential that the child grows in self-esteem and self-love; it is important for the child to know about his neighbors, local, national, and international; students must understand and appreciate the wonders of nature; they must learn how to get along with others and to cooperate with them in making this a better world; students must know as much as possible about nature and be good stewards; children must actively live in and belong to the city, the state, and the nation by being good citizens; and they must listen to the Church, believe in its mission, and follow faithfully its teaching by being good Catholics. The most important relationship, however, is the one with God. As creatures, boys and girls (men and women) must know as much as possible about this relationship, and they must live and behave in the light of such knowledge.

Each person, then, has a special relationship with God, with his Church, with his neighbor, with nature, and with himself. Children must understand that only one thing can destroy this relationship with God and this is deliberate violation of God's laws — sin — and sin can be erased by sorrow and forgiveness. Jesus summarized all this for us when He taught "You shall love the Lord your God with all your heart and all your soul and all your strength and all your mind, and your neighbor as yourself."[7]

INTEGRATION.[8] Catholic educators add a second ingredient, integration, equally important with religion for Catholic Education. The student must learn to integrate these great religious truths with every other phase of life. This begins at birth but especially in school where the student begins to learn how to integrate the most fundamental truth of all with other parts of the curriculum. Truths about Religion, God and His Church, the child's neighbors and himself, and love become the *core* of the curriculum for the Catholic schools. John Dewey[9] wanted the entire curriculum to enrich and take meaning from the idea of "good citizenship," or "growth," and this core idea would ultimately guide everything else in the curriculum. For Dewey, good citizenship and growth became the master (core) ideas, the final arbiter and interpreter of the entire curriculum, the principal idea for the understanding and interpretation of life itself.

In the Catholic school this unique core idea is God and the truths He has given us to live this life properly. For example, the child must understand that one must be a good citizen or he is failing not only man's expectations and laws, but also those of God. The child is not a good neighbor if he or she is not a good child of God. When one studies science he must be led to discover the great truths about reality; to search for the laws that regulate the world and its parts, as well as the earth and heavenly bodies; to understand to the extent possible the many mysteries of life in the universe. The student must also understand that these laws, these relationships, these mysteries were not designed by men. Men merely discovered them and named them. The student must be led to understand that there is a Supreme Intelligence that made and directs everything in the universe. This is God. Johnson's Course of Studies gives a brief survey of the scope of integration.[10]

Such integration of the key principles of life must not only help us understand life better; it must also guide and motivate us to live better. For example, we must understand that being a good neighbor is not just the decent thing to do, it is required by God's plan. Certainly we can be punished for not serving our country, but more serious is the fact that we are obliged to love our country and be loyal and faithful to it by the plan of God. This is God's justice put into practice. "Render to Caesar the things that are Caesar's and to God the things that are God's."[11]

Students must study carefully every subject in the curriculum and, in so far as possible, understand them. Catholic education is not as some may think simply the study of religious truths. Each subject must be carefully integrated, understood, and related with the truths that God has given, the core truths. One part of life must not be isolated from the other if the whole of life is to be properly understood.

Integration may be the most important subject in the Course of Studies. Without a doubt it takes a very skilled and well-informed teacher to understand the role of integration in the education of the child.

RELIGION'S PLACE IN THE SCHOOL. Finally there is a third characteristic for Catholic education. It cannot properly be called subject matter but it does belong with what has already been said. It has to do with the actual teaching of religion.

Chapter 3 – Catholic Philosophy and the Curriculum

One unfortunately discovers that Religion often takes the very last place in the school schedule: it is the first subject dropped or shortened when something "important" crops up in the school day like a "fire drill." Religion must be treated with at least the same respect that every other subject in the course of studies receives. Some schools, because of the heavy schedule required, will resort to extreme measures to meet the time requirements of other subjects. In this process religion is often reduced a few periods a week.

The need for qualified personnel is another important consideration in the teaching of religion. A poorly prepared religion teacher can be a disaster in that subject as is any poorly prepared teacher in any subject. Religion requires a properly prepared and qualified teacher. In fact, since religious education is the primary purpose of the Catholic school, the religion class deserves to be the best taught subject in the curriculum, and to have the very best teacher available. Some administrators have very wisely assigned religious instruction to teachers who also carry another important "secular" subject. This can have a beneficial effect on the student as well as the teacher.

In the so-called secular areas, the number of periods and minutes is standardized and often determined by State regulations. Thus, the school and the State are telling the student something important: these subjects are very necessary for one's education and to do them properly sufficient time will be required. One notices how school authorities require so many days and hours in the schedule. When something makes this impossible the time must be made up even if it would mean attending class on scheduled holidays.

Religious education deserves nothing less. The student must learn that religion is the most important subject in the curriculum.

Can you imagine what an impact the exclusion of religion from the curriculum must have on the mind of the child? This tells the child that religion is not important, certainly not as important as other subjects. If you can get through school without it, so can one get through life without it. The place of religion in the life of the students tells dramatically whether it is important or not. This is the clear message of the public school.

Some have said this is a responsibility which must be entrusted to the Church or parents. To those who would say that, please note that parents are responsible for the entire education of the child, not just religion. The importance of treating religion with the same seriousness as other subjects is one of the great advantages of the Catholic school.

Children need time to grasp the content of religion and they must understand the importance of the subject itself.

Catholic education has already made a judgment, throughout a long and difficult history, about the importance of Religion in life. Until that judgment can be honestly made, one cannot properly nor ultimately make an intelligent decision about the time and space religion deserves in school. Better perhaps than many people,

Catholics should understand that such judgments must be made. One can be justly enraged when people decide that religion is not as important as other subjects in the curriculum and therefore really deserves no attention in the school.

Teachers know that religious judgments are made all the time and in every subject. Who could teach the history of any nation without discussing the "right" or "wrong," the "good" or "bad" of certain events? The Holocaust, slavery, the Civil War, the World Wars, Racism, to mention only a few examples. All these events and many others involve important religious and moral truths that must be acknowledged and explained. Important judgments must be made in every area of life. To avoid such judgment does not achieve the neutrality that certain eminent lawyers and philosophers are seeking between Church and State. It does leave a great void in the education of a child.

REFLECTION

Vatican II warned that "today's progress in science and technology can foster a certain exclusive emphasis on observable data, and an agnosticism about everything else."[12] The warning was most timely. Advances made in science and technology in the 20th century have been spectacular. However, such progress often comes at a very high price.

As the Council noted, such extraordinary development tends to highlight science and technology as the mother of all truth. At the same time it tends to submerge other disciplines such as religion, philosophy, history, and the fine arts.[13]

During the twentieth century science and technology have surpassed all other disciplines, and these subjects clearly carried the day in the areas of new knowledge, achievement, and progress.

But such advances do not exclude the possibility of serious problems. In fact, their achievements, without other disciplines to check, correct, and limit their enthusiasm, can sometimes be very harmful. The second world war climaxed with the explosion of atomic bombs over Nagasaki and Hiroshima. Those mighty bombs were the direct product of twentieth century science and technology. The world never before witnessed such scientific achievements nor the exercise of such power. The tragic destruction resulting may have brought an end to a terrible war, but it also exercised power never before known and destruction beyond imagination. It clearly taught that modern warfare, with its advanced technology and science, should seek and heed knowledge available from other disciplines. Modern warfare is now so savage that one must ask whether war as it is actually waged today can be morally justified.[14]

The protest of such devastating use of power has been long and loud. One immediate result was the issuance of a statement by the NCCB in 1976 stating that such modern weapons must not be used.

"As possessors of a vast nuclear arsenal we must also be aware that it is not only wrong to attack civilian population but it is also wrong to threaten them even when this is a part of a strategy of deterrence. Since that time many have attempted to get greater control over those weapons and ultimately remove them entirely."[15]

Not everyone agreed with the position of the bishops. Get rid of the nuclear weapons? — yes, but only if they do not belong to our arsenal. In the meantime new nuclear weapons have appeared on schedule and as promised more destructive and more terrible. The discussions on these new weapons continues on and on.

Science and technology have also brought us to the brink of an even greater disaster. It all began when the two disciplines tried to do something about childless parents. In vitro fertilization after all seemed harmless enough. It would be used to do what nature, unaided, was failing to do.

Regretfully this noble goal soon deteriorated. It has become, in fact, a threat to the family by its availability to displace that sacred bond within which the family should be created and in which it is to grow and develop. Now "in vitro" has become the toy for many who reject marriage, for homosexuals who want their relationship to resemble the family which they are anxious to displace. Even though same sex unions cannot make new life, science and technology is ready, willing, and able to do so.

One thing leads to another and it seemed inevitable that a new technology would soon appear — cloning. The lovable "Dolly" may be the first in a long line of clones which could be used to replace a beloved child, or to placate an empty family with adoptees, or even to provide a fertile field for reaping organs that have a tendency to go bad.

The Church has again tried to bring the presence of other disciplines into this potential social volcano. Each child deserves and has a right to a family and should be the fruit of the special love between husband and wife. Children should not be the product of bizarre production or "wholesale" like distribution. God's way is not man's way; if there is any concern about society, then the family and new life must be preserved.

One can only imagine what in vitro fertilization and cloning might lead to. Some theologians are already warning that these "products" — these off-springs without families — are entitled to all the rights, privileges, and responsibilities accorded every human being.

The real danger is that such unbridled progress in science and technology will continue. The old saw must be remembered: if it can be done, it will be done sooner or later.

Somehow in this war of disciplines, all must understand that because a thing can be done, there is no reason that it must be done, especially if other limitations exist. Those limitations are discovered by study of other fields and arts: history, philosophy, fine arts and religion.

Education will play a leading role in this struggle against cloning human life in the war against the family.

The role of science and technology must be respected. Each child should know how these disciplines have made extraordinary progress. But students must know other things as well. It must be understood that while producing great wonders, they cannot "give the whole truth" nor can these sciences "penetrate to the ultimate meaning of things." These warnings of Vatican II deserve recognition. "Yet the danger exists that man, confiding too much in modern discoveries, may even think that he is sufficient unto himself and no longer seeks any higher realities."[16]

These examples underline the importance of integration where the meaning and use of a reality or a discovery would be more completely understood and properly limited by its relationship to the core truths of the curriculum as explained in the opening pages of this chapter. Likewise, "…the various disciplines of philosophy, of history, of the fine arts must be seriously undertaken and become vehicles to elevate the human family to a more sublime understanding of truth, goodness and beauty, and to the formation of judgments which concern values. Thus, mankind can be more clearly enlightened by that marvelous Wisdom which was with God from all eternity."[17]

NOTES

1) Quigley, T.J., McDowell, J.B., Handbook of School Policies and Practices (Diocese of Pittsburgh [rev.] 1947, published for local use only), 16, 17.

2) ibid., School Curriculum, 20.

3) ibid., 17,18.

4) Johnson, George, Guiding Growth in Christian Social Living, 3 vols. (Washington, D.C., Catholic University Press, 1946 - 1952).

5) ibid., Vol. 1, 9-14.

6) Johnson, George, Better Men for Better Times (Washington, D.C., Catholic University Press, 1943).

7) Luke 10:27.

8) Integration has quite a different meaning in today's society than when George Johnson wrote. In Johnson's sense it means the unification or integrity of secular subjects in and with religion.

9) Dewey, 51.

10) Johnson, Guiding Growth in Christian Living, 102-108 ff.

11) Matthew 22:20.

12) Walter Abbott, S.J., "The Church Today," The Documents of Vatican II (New York, America Press, 1966) II, 57.

13) ibid., II, 57.

14) "To Live in Christ Jesus" (NCCB, Washington, D.C., 1976), 34.

15) ibid., 34.

16) Abbott, op. cit., II, 57.

17) ibid., II, 57.

CHAPTER 4

Catholic School Leaders

Although Catholic education has had the longest history in education in America, it had no great individual leaders except for certain Bishops who took it upon themselves as teachers of the Catholic flock to do what had to be done. Great names like John Carroll, John Hughes, James Cardinal Gibbons, John Spalding, and John England were among those great men who were part of the development of American Catholic education.

Tribute is paid as one of the great Catholic educators to Bishop John Nepomucene Neumann (1811-1860). He was one of the many bishops in early United States to have a significant interest and influence on education. His influence began when he joined the Redemptorist Community and became Vice Provincial of that Religious Order. In 1852 he was appointed Bishop of Philadelphia and again in that capacity he showed an intense interest in parochial school education. Both as a member of the Redemptorist Community and as a Bishop of a Diocese, he became prominent because of his concern for parochial schools and about their diocesan-wide organization. His reputation was widely spread as a diligent developer of parish schools. When he died suddenly in 1860, his cause for beatification was almost immediately instituted, and in 1977 he was declared a Saint of the Church by Pope John Paul II.

These Bishops had special abilities but few of them had any special training in education, especially at the elementary or secondary levels. Bishops in the early nineteenth century simply had to do certain things in order to provide for the education and protection of the faith of the children and adults in their flock. At every level of education Bishops were active in providing Catholic education programs for the millions of Catholics coming to the new land. They took this responsibility simply because it had to be done.

Some, however, were chosen by the Bishops to supervise the education of the people. Some have been truly outstanding Catholic educators.

MONSIGNOR GEORGE JOHNSON (1889-1944)[1]

One of the greatest American Catholic educators was George Johnson, born in Toledo, Ohio in 1889. After attending school in the States, he was sent to the North American College in Rome, where he studied Theology and was ordained a priest at the age of twenty-five in 1914. When he was thirty years old his Bishop sent him to earn the Doctorate in Education at the Catholic University of America. Upon his return to Toledo he served as Superintendent of Catholic Schools in that Diocese from 1919 until 1921. In that year he was appointed Professor of Education at Catholic University of America. He remained at this post until his sudden and unexpected death in 1944. From 1921 to 1924 Johnson lived away from the University in a local Parish where he was in charge of the parish Catholic elementary school. In 1925 Catholic University established its own elementary school known as the Campus School, and George Johnson was appointed Director. In 1928 and 1929 he was appointed the Director of the Department of Education of the Catholic Bishops Organization, the NCWC (now NCCB). At the same time, he was appointed the Secretary General of the National Catholic Educational Association, a professional organization for the Catholic teachers and administrators of the nation.

In 1938 Johnson was appointed Dean of the School of Education at Catholic University but he held that post for only two years. He was involved in so many other Catholic educational programs that he had little time for anything except getting out his important message. From the time of his appointment in 1921 he held the post of Professor of Education in the Graduate School of Education until his untimely death.

Pope Pius XI, who had intense interest in Catholic Education, wrote a letter of congratulations to the University on its fiftieth year of educational work (1939). After pointing out that "Christian Doctrine and Christian Morality are under attack from several quarters," the Holy Father went on to express his desire that Catholic University would undertake special programs for the education of Catholic people, especially to help them understand, from a Christian point of view, the privileges and the responsibilities of American citizenship. In response to this request the Rector of the University established a Committee known as the Commission on American Citizenship and Monsignor Johnson was named to its Executive Committee. In 1943 he was named Director of the Commission and published that same year with Father Robert Slavin, O.P., his first masterful work *Better Men for Better Times.* This became the blueprint for a new era in Catholic education in America. In that same year Johnson's classic work *Guiding Growth in Christian Social Living* was complete in outline form and the first volume was published.

Monsignor Johnson would not be living when the other two volumes were completed, but his directions of what was to be done and his outline of the entire work were so clear that his very capable successor, Monsignor Frederick Hochwalt, ably supervised the completion of volumes II and III, which were published in 1946. This work gave a detailed picture of elementary education from grades 1 to 8, and provided a model curriculum based on the Catholic philosophy of education. Most important, this work integrated the Core Curriculum with every subject at every elementary level. It was an extraordinary work and indicates in a special way Johnson's extensive knowledge of education and the proper role of religion in the curriculum.

Unfortunately Monsignor Johnson was stricken while giving a graduation talk in June 1944 and died at the age of 55.

What great things this man accomplished for Catholic education! As Director of the Department of Education, NCWC, he was entrusted with assisting the Bishops to formulate important statements of policy and conveying their messages to the people and educators of this country. His most important position was as Secretary General of the National Catholic Educational Association. Through this position teachers, principals, and superintendents became familiar with this noted educator and were influenced by his inspirational knowledge of Catholic education, American style. The interesting details of his writings on the curriculum of Catholic schools have been given in the previous chapter. His book *Better Men for Better Times* concerned the relationship of Catholic philosophy and American citizenship. "Christian teaching alone, in its majestic integrity, can give full meaning and compelling motive to the demands for human rights and liberties because it alone gives worth and dignity to human personality." These words were taken from Pope Pius XI's congratulatory letter to Catholic University and they became the theme of the book which Monsignor Johnson wrote on Catholic education. Throughout this extraordinary text Johnson emphasized that the most sacred thing under the sun is the individual human personality.

His association with the Superintendents of Catholic Schools throughout the nation was particularly significant. These were the men who would be entrusted by their Bishops with implementing and developing the Catholic concept of education in the individual dioceses throughout the nation. Many of these superintendents had been students of Monsignor Johnson; some did their doctoral work under his direction; all of them were familiar with his writings and works.

The superintendents, the bishops' education experts, were the local link between Monsignor Johnson, the professor, the director of the NCEA, the educational chief of the NCWC, and the local pastors, supervisors, principals, teachers, students and their parents. With the implementation and adoption of "Guiding Growth" as the official plan for Catholic education programs throughout the land, Catholic schools were on their way to their golden era.

In 1950 the Catholic school population, elementary and secondary, exceeded 2.5 million students. Twenty years later it would be 4.0 million students in the United States alone.[2]

What the superintendents accomplished for Catholic education in the forties and fifties was extraordinary and is gratefully acknowledged. They were carefully and skillfully prepared educators. Individually and together they organized the Catholic schools of each diocese into a smoothly working educational operation. They took the program prepared by Monsignor Johnson and made it the framework of the education of Catholic children throughout the nation. They saw to it that relevant state laws were observed in the Catholic schools: they dealt with the appropriate state officials; they kept diocesan programmers informed about the latest trends in education and regularly met with local teachers and administrators to assure-that their little section of the vineyard was up to date.

For those superintendents, Monsignor Johnson was an extraordinary leader. His writings, his addresses, his teaching and administrative skills, and his awareness after personal experience with the role and problems of the diocesan superintendent of schools, made him not only a great leader for these educators, but also a tremendous inspiration and influence in the cause of Catholic life and education throughout the nation.

THE CATHOLIC SCHOOL RELIGIOUS[3]

The teaching religious of the late thirties, the forties, the fifties, and early sixties, were the pride of the Catholic school system. From the very beginning the religious teachers, both women and men, have played a key role in the establishment and development of American Catholic schools. Actually the first Catholic school teachers were lay people, but as time went on, more and more religious became available to staff Catholic elementary and secondary schools. What they accomplished is incredible.

Many of these Religious Communities came from abroad. In fact, many of them accompanied communities of their own people to the shores of this land. They went with them into the cities and towns which would be home for the new immigrants. There the religious helped establish school programs for the education of their children. This was especially the pattern in the case of those immigrants who did not speak English. In some cases teachers and children learned a new language and culture together.

There was another arrangement that took over not long after the religious arrival into America. It was caused by the Americanization of these Religious Communities along with the people. They began to attract vocations from among the local population. After a few years, when the original members of the group passed on, the Americanized members dominated the Community. They did not desert the original establishments but rather they helped them become a working part of the local and national scene. In the meantime the growth of these Communities made it possible to spread their influence and to found new convents and new schools.

Another plan must be mentioned: the American Foundation of Religious. Typical of this pattern were the Sisters of Charity. Their story reads like a novel.

Elizabeth Bayley[4] was born in New York City on August 28, 1774. She came from a distinguished Colonial family. Her father was a physician and a medical professor, and the family was prominent in local society and in the Episcopal Church. Elizabeth's early training was directed by her father, her mother having died when she was very young. In her youth biographers tell us she was deeply religious and showed a particular concern and affection for the poor and the sick.

In 1794 she married a young, wealthy merchant by the name of William Magee Seton, and they became the parents of five children. Her biographers tell us that her husband eventually lost his great wealth and at the same time his health. In an attempt to help him recover, Elizabeth took him to Italy where they lived with some friends who had a great influence on their life.

Elizabeth's husband died at Pisa after six weeks in Italy. After a brief stay with her friends, Elizabeth returned to New York. Then in 1805 she converted to Catholicism and with her children began a new life. She took over an abandoned school which was near St. Mary's Seminary in Baltimore, Maryland. There she would be near her friend, Father William Dubourg, Superior of the Baltimore Sulpicians. A number of young ladies came to this new girls school to assist Elizabeth. Meanwhile Father Dubourg, with the help of Archbishop John Carroll of Baltimore, decided after careful thought and prayer, to invite Elizabeth and her friends to the Sisterhood. Dubourg received her vows and gave her the title of Mother. It was then that the distinctive habit of the Sisters of Charity came into existence.

Students of Elizabeth Seton's life tell us that she moved to Emmitsburg, Maryland and established the Motherhouse. They also state that during these years she laid the foundation for the American parochial school system. It is known that she prepared teachers and wrote textbooks; many were translations from the French.

Mother Elizabeth Seton was an extraordinary woman and religious. Catholic education in America owes this extraordinary religious woman a great debt. Scholars maintain that Elizabeth Seton was the real genius behind the parochial school.

What has been given above concerning the life of Mother Elizabeth Seton is only a brief summary. Many books have been written about her life and these are recommended to those who want to know more about the interesting details of this extraordinary life.[5]

On Sunday morning, September 14, 1975, in the presence of some hundreds of thousands of people gathered in St. Peter's Square, Pope Paul VI spoke particularly to some 20 thousand American citizens:

"We rejoice and we are deeply moved that our apostolic ministry authorizes us to make this solemn declaration before all of you here present, before the Holy Catholic Church, before our other Christian brethren in the world, before the entire American people, and before all humanity, Elizabeth Ann Bailey Seton is a Saint. She is the first daughter of the United States of America to be glorified with this incomparable attribute."[6]

Sister Marie Celeste, S.C. wrote a wonderful book about this great Saint from which we have quoted her recording of that beautiful ceremony in Vatican City. She goes on to write: "In the history of the United States and of the Catholic Church, Elizabeth Ann Bailey Seton is unique. With her many roles as wife, mother, socialite and friend, widow, educator and the foundress of a Religious Community, she is an apt model of American womanhood for the universal church."[7]

Since Elizabeth Seton's death in 1821, thousands of young women have become Sisters of Charity and they have established many parochial schools throughout this country. Most recently a convent and a school were established in Korea and some of the first Korean Sisters of Charity have come to the United States to complete their studies.

The story of the Sisters of Charity is unique because that Community is native to this country. Most Communities are not. The Mercy Nuns, for example, sent seven Sisters from Ireland, who managed to attract many American young ladies to their Community. The growth was impressive. This same phenomenon happened to the Franciscans and their many branches. The Josephites and Divine Providence Religious had similar experiences. These and other Communities, while looking to another nation for their roots, came to America, established a Motherhouse and in time drew hundreds of young ladies to their way of life. Once well established they reached out, staffed parish schools throughout the country, and made their greatest impact in Catholic education and the health care areas.

Over 70% of Religious Communities[8] have their roots in other countries and came to the United States as missionaries. Remarkably, in a few years after their establishment in this country all of them were receiving new members. This indicated their acceptance by the American people and, more important, it indicated that the Sisters had accepted the people in this new land.

Nationally there are more than 400 different women religious communities and all but a small percentage were involved in one way or another in the Catholic educational program. What a treasure. The Sisters made ideal teachers. All but a few engaged in teaching lived in convents on the same property with the school where they were assigned. There they made their home. If they were away from that convent it was only during the summer months or because they were needed elsewhere. The convent became the nerve center of all the local Catholic-inspired educational activities.

Sisters rose early in the morning; together they said their morning prayers, attended Mass, and received Holy Communion; had their breakfast together; then off to their classrooms. At the end of the day they again came together for prayer. In most convents they prepared their lessons, studied for the next day, or corrected papers in a common room. In all they would spend several hours in such a room preparing their lessons. This was done with the same seriousness as they said their prayers. Every day ended the same way. They would gather in the Chapel, recite their night prayers, and then off to their own room for the night. Thus, Religious Congregations offered a life of spirituality with a promise of its further development, and they blended this with a career in teaching the children, not only the skills required for living, but those also required to attain eternal life. The combination of the religious life with the teaching life made an ideal blend and Religious Communities attracted not only those that were deeply interested in improving their spiritual life but those as well who wanted to do something about the education of youth.

All those who entered the Sisterhood had to spend a period of postulancy — a period to test their suitability for the life they had chosen to live and during which they and their Superiors evaluated their suitability. They would spend at least a year in the novitiate; an intensive period of prayer and spiritual preparation, and then off to school, although many spent their days in hospitals, orphanages, and other dedicated service. At an appropriate time they took vows — poverty, chastity, obedience. These vows have been the bedrock of the Religious life for centuries. At first the vows were temporary, but when the candidates were ready, they took their vows for life.

With such a preparation as a foundation, the religious spent their lives in prayer, in study, in teaching, in learning, in serving others, and in more prayer. This was the routine of the life of the Sisters in the Golden Era. What ideal conditions for a teacher. They were not hyphenated people; they were not Sister-teachers. Their lives as teachers and religious blended together as one like Monsignor Johnson's integrated curriculum. They lived as religious in and out of the classroom. What an extraordinary situation. What wonderful days for the Church and the world.

Many men also belong to religious communities. Some of those religious are priests and some are brothers; some spent their lives teaching; some were assigned to other apostolates. About 15% of the religious men taught in the Catholic school system. They constituted a significant number of Catholic teachers and their lives were very similar to those of the religious women. Their lives were composed of vows, prayer, study, service, and teaching.

These religious women and men made extraordinary contributions to the Church and to the nation. They were in the front lines of the Catholic educational program. Because they lived together, prayed together, and taught together, they became ideal communities in which the younger members were helped, inspired, and guided by the older, more experienced religious. There is no way that we could possibly acknowledge what these religious have done for Catholic education and the Church and accomplished as religious under the direction of the Church. They were an inspiration, not only to the youngsters, but to their parents, and, indeed, to the entire adult community.

This endowment is no longer available in such significant numbers as it once was. Beginning in the 1960's the number of teaching religious, both women and men, was suddenly reduced.[9] The decline in religious has been disastrous: 80,883 Sisters and 5,297 Brothers. For the sisters, it was a loss of 2,247 members a year; 186 members a month; or 5 members every single day in a 36-year period. The brothers, during a 26-year period, lost 158 members a year or about 13 members a month. Unbelievable? Nevertheless, it is true, and many who find those numbers difficult to accept and wonder why this happened are trying to find out what did actually happen. When things happened like this centuries ago there was always some political reason — a royal decree giving the time and date for the departure of a religious community. Not so this time and many are beginning to wonder just what caused this tragic decline.

As terrible as this erosion of religious life in our country, the decline of Catholic elementary and secondary school population was even more devastating. Beginning in the late sixties that decline set in and the population of the Catholic schools is only now beginning to settle down. The National Catholic Education Association issued the following data:

CATHOLIC SCHOOL ELEMENTARY AND SECONDARY ENROLLMENT 1960:
all Catholic secondary schools	844,295
all Catholic elementary schools	4,275,896
	5,120,191

CATHOLIC SCHOOL ELEMENTARY AND SECONDARY ENROLLMENT 1996:
all Catholic secondary schools	647,613
all Catholic elementary schools	2,052,193
	2,699,806

DECLINE: ELEMENTARY AND SECONDARY:
1960 - 1996:	2,420,385

The total drop in Catholic elementary and secondary school enrollment in a period of 36 years was an amazing 2,420,385, or an average of 67,232 annually. More than 75 entire schools disappeared annually.

Any wonder that many concerned scholars are looking into this devastating situation? What an extraordinary phenomenon. In less than 36 years more than 80,000 Sisters, 5,000 Brothers, and 2.4 million students left the parochial schools at the elementary and secondary levels. Any wonder that there was such great concern? At first sight it appears to be some sort of statistical error. Yet these are cold facts, and this situation deserves to be carefully investigated. What did happen?

Ann Carey[10], a correspondent with *Our Sunday Visitor*, wrote a book recently entitled *Sisters in Crisis: The Tragic Unraveling of Women's Religious Communities* and gave her insights into the crisis. She maintains that radical reformers went far beyond what the Church had asked in Vatican II and "devastated" the basic elements of religious life. Carey takes a long look at "a new attribute of individualism" which is a frequent criticism made of the recent renewal of religious life. One who is infected with "Individualism" is hardly prepared to contribute anything to "Community" life which is one of the essential elements of religious life. Carey also claims that many Religious leaders of reform had accepted radical feminism as a philosophy of life and that most of the radical changes can be traced to about ten change-oriented Sisters.

In recent months several thought-provoking reviews of Carey's book have appeared. One came from Father Kenneth Baker, S.J.[11], Editor of *Pastoral and Homiletic*

Review and a respected priest and reliable writer on such matters as renewal and other Catholic concerns. His analysis is that "These feminist Nuns were highly organized, politically astute and they had clear goals: substitute personal choice for obedience and Community life, declare their independency from Rome and the hierarchy, disband large Communities, eliminate Community commitments such as schools, and adopt a secular life style in dress, work, and living arrangement."

Monsignor George A. Kelly, a New York priest and former professor at St. John's University, also reviewed Carey's book which he found very brave and outspoken. Like Father Baker, Monsignor Kelly[12] believed that the "Reformers" of the Religious were at fault and gives names. In his review he cites one Sister, laicized in 1995, and eight priests active in renewal work, whom he charges with the decline in religious life. He also states in the same review that there were "tightly organized meetings of selected religious, sometimes held in secret; assemblies with one-sided speakers;…episcopal and Roman letters withheld from the troops," and on and on.

Religious women generally have denounced Ann Carey's book. They also refused to accept that feminist Sisters conspired to attack religious communities. Nevertheless, something terrible happened which caused this disaster. One detects, many say, what seems like a highly organized and methodical dismantling of religious life. Its future in America is bleak.

Other explanations have been offered for this tragic decrease in religious community membership. It has been said that the evils of the past forty years have done very little to stimulate vocations or even to encourage continuance of religious life. Such evils include consumerism, hedonism, permissiveness, individualism, personalism, and the widespread acceptance of secularism, naturalism, and certainly there is evidence of feminism among Sisters, both the moderate version and the extreme.

Those who have considered the recent damage wonder how it would be possible, with such evils so prevelant and so firmly established in our society, to live even a moderately good life let alone a committed spiritual life. One must admit the presence of these evil influences, and accept the fact they are more evident and influential in the lives of individuals than ever before. Movies, television, novels, magazines constantly breathe out these evils. The effects of this moral filth are evident in the modern American lifestyle. Its influence on the lives of the young, and even the more mature, is sadly but dramatically evident.

It seems almost impossible to continue a young person's interest in religious life when such evil confronts them. This may explain, to an extent, why there are few — often none — applying for religious life today. This false picture of what life is all about (so attractively packaged) makes religious life seem dull and uninteresting.

Yet this is what religious life is all about: to provide the interior life of grace and the strength to face the evils of the age.

The change to lay garb had a sobering effect on the faithful and the religious.

Many unfortunately read into this a major change in religious lifestyle. They were not prepared for this sudden and drastic change. At first there was the traditional religious garb and suddenly it had been replaced by lay dress. The preparation made by the religious themselves left much to be desired. To early questions about these changes in dress the answer came back that it was "Just experimental." The final "modified" garb reduced the religious dress, an important and familiar external symbol of religious life, to forms of clothing that had little or no reference to what the religious represented. Of course their life was to manifest what the garb once represented. It was difficult for most to understand. At the beginning most of the faithful were expecting a modified garb which had been "modeled" for "moments" during the period of change.

One Superior told me, "I don't understand, 'they' told me if we went to lay dress we would not be able to keep the applicants out. We haven't had a vocation since that time." "They" were not identified.

But whoever or whatever engineered these changes made clear that the religious life was the target. An elderly and proven Religious responded to my inquiry that Community life was an early victim. "Every religious, whatever his or her apostolic work, must normally live under the authority of a local Superior in a community of the Institute to which he or she belongs."[13] That, of course, said one former Religious, was before religious began to live alone or in small groups in apartments. Currently there are far too many living in apartments without sufficient reason. Apartment living is simply not a substitute for Community life. Remember "the capacity to live Community life (is) a quality which distinguishes a religious vocation to a given institute and is a key criteria of suitability in a candidate."[14]

The vows did not escape, explained a seventy-year-old Sister. Obedience took a beating. Explanations by "experts" almost did away with this vow completely and turned it into a kind of optional negotiation. Its true meaning was clear: obedience is a religious pledge to obey the directives of the lawful Superior.[15]

Obedience is the keystone of religious life. But what if there were no Superiors? Soon something like that is exactly what happened. The LCWR (not to be confused with the Institute on Religious Life) had already declared its autonomy from the hierarchy several years ago. Now their leaders repudiated the Roman Documents on Religious Life. By using new labels — First Minister — Leadership Committee — Chairperson — President — etc. — several problems suddenly disappeared. Humility, it was maintained, demanded the elimination of such unwanted and "inappropriate" terms as "Mother" or "Superior." Obedience gradually waned. As religious life began to crumble it became much easier to say that there could be no Community commitments.

No doubt our values have declined since the sixties. Many like to point to Vatican II and say — there is the cause of all this. A recent document issued by the Holy See[16] gives a special insight into how Vatican II was often made the scapegoat for our present problems. The word came out that "experts" said it was so; the Congregation for Religious does not understand American Apostolic Religious; non-ordained can give the homily; extraordinary ministers may distribute Holy Communion at any time; women religious can be pastors; some non-ordained were already wearing the vestments and "concelebrating" Mass.

The Document told the story in a different light. What this important Roman Document revealed was that such aberrations were never approved by any Roman Congregation. They were created by non-officials, individuals or groups, who just thought they would be improvements. They were suggested by some priests, religious, or laity who made themselves "experts" in the affairs of Vatican II.

At the time of the famous Listening Sessions in 1973, there was a clear pattern emerging. By that time the dismantling was underway. One constantly recurring theme was that the Roman Documents were wonderful but they simply did not apply to American religious life. The Roman Congregation did not understand the religious of the United States. The rules were written for European, monastic (cloistered) type religious, not for apostolic religious in America.

Therefore they could agree with Essential Elements in full. What it had to say simply did not apply to life in American convents.

These changes in the lifestyle of the religious initiated an unfortunate response from the laity. One Religious, in good standing, stated that young ladies who formerly would have been potential vocations openly rejected this new lifestyle and made it clear that "one could live that sort of life without joining a religious community." Apparently numerous potential vocations responded in precisely that way.

Most religious do not know why all this happened. Some do have interesting thoughts about what happened. Such information comes from proven, clearly committed, mature and intelligent religious women who, by the way, openly question the Ann Carey story.

Religious communities do have great problems, they say. Feminists do belong to religious communities. Some can be extreme, but the majority are what they call normal or moderate feminists. Sisters generally complain about the male domination of women religious life. They believe greater representation of women is needed at the top levels. But, they say, these are not the kind of women who would march on Rome or start a riot. Yes, there are some extreme feminists in religious life but, they maintain, not of the Ann Carey type.

Solid religious were concerned more about the "professional" women, namely, the well-educated and degreed religious, well read and elegant mannered, whose commitment to being "professional" seemed obviously greater than to the religious life. These could be the ones who like apartment life and often opt for it. Many mature religious believe that apartment life, when unnecessary, has done the greatest damage to Religious, because this was a direct attack on community life. These committed religious also admit and regret what has happened to obedience; they do not accept recent interpretations of that vow. Some refer to it as the "theologian's toy."

Finally, they feel that some rules of religious life were too rigid (some were labeled inhumane); and they agreed that changes were needed. But it was a case of too much, too quickly. Surprisingly, I never heard any Sisters from the group indicated attempt, beyond what was said above, any further explanation of the disastrous decline or the lack of vocations. Both these facts are a mystery to most of them. Perhaps, they muse, less tempestuous feminists; more religiously committed professionals; more understanding and patient bishops and priests; a more available Roman Congregation would have made a difference. These Sisters also expressed a real need to have more local ecclesiastical control.

The final paragraphs of this amazing mystery story have not been written. Nevertheless it can be said, no matter what the real story, there is plenty of guilt and responsibility to be shared among the religious, the congregations, the clergy, the bishops, and perhaps even the laity.

However this episode began, it has seriously crippled religious life. Fortunately some were not overcome by this unhappy event. For those remaining, it is improbable that what was known as religious life, which did so much good, will ever be seen or experienced again.

Sisters who were in many cases unaware of what was going on (and there were many) will still enjoy a happy life if the faithful, priests, bishops and laity have anything to say about it. The annual Sisters' Retirement Collection is one visible sign of this. So many miss what they had — especially the life of prayer and service which they had freely chosen. They need our help and they will receive it.

Catholic elementary and secondary schools have experienced a serious blow. Of course there will always be a few to remind us of what might have happened to education in this country. Whether Catholic education can recover from this near fatal blow remains to be seen.

We pray that there will be other great women and men raised up who will restore religious life and establish new ways of bringing the young into the service of the Lord and His Church.

We can say without hesitation that the Religious women and men, who were engaged in the teaching apostolate of the Church, did an extraordinary and noble job. Certainly the years they were involved in such great numbers were Golden Years for the Church and its educational program in America. We will never be able to thank them. And it is unlikely that the Golden Years will occur again.

What the future of the Catholic schools will be remains to be seen. What was developed over a period of 150 years by the toil of dedicated bishops, laity and devoted religious cannot be supplemented instantaneously. For the present the Church must look to the lay teachers if its educational apostolate is to continue. As a matter of fact, forty years ago, there were 13,400 lay teachers serving in Catholic schools throughout the country. Since the decline in the number of religious teachers, that number of lay teachers has risen to 152,165.[17] That the schools were able to make such sweeping changes in less than forty years despite such difficult times in

Church and in society is almost incredible. Today the lay teachers are the main force in our Catholic schools. Most recently a new President for the National Catholic Educational Association was elected. For the first time in history, it is not a priest nor a sister, but a layman.

Since Vatican II, when great changes began in our schools and throughout the Church, lay people have been called upon to be more involved in the actual operation of the Church. The teachers in our Catholic schools are only one example of how they have responded.

It is too soon to say whether or not this great change in our school program will have positive outcomes. To date all is going well. Lay teachers have taken their role as teachers and administrators in the schools with great seriousness. In their national meetings they have discussed the problems which this change would create. They have emphasized the importance of bringing to the classroom a true witness of personal holiness if the goals of Catholic education are to be achieved. We look to the laity with great confidence. They have the future of Catholic education and Catholic children in their hands.

In discussing the leadership of Catholic schools in this country, tribute must be paid to so many priests serving our parishes. The school succeeds to the extent that the priests are in favor of the program and demonstrate their support publicly. Good pastors for years — indeed from the beginning — have done everything to keep the schools alive. This involved personal sacrifices and leadership almost beyond imagination, including everything from the famous bingo parties to the inevitable raffles. These pastors became known as "School-men." Indeed they are.

As we salute the leaders of Catholic education in this country, we give a special salute and utter a silent prayer for the "School-men," past and present, who did so much for Catholic education.

CONCLUSION

Catholic education had its share of great men and women who sacrificed for the good of the schools. The religious women and men, the founders of religious communities such as Mother Elizabeth Seton, the Catholic school superintendents, Monsignor George Johnson, and the bishops of the nation, the great priest "School-Men" — their unselfish work and sacrifices should ever be acknowledged and gratefully remembered in each classroom of each Catholic school and home in this land. All this has been made possible because of the unselfish generosity of the laity who have supported in every way possible the countless efforts and programs undertaken by the Church for the love of their schools and children.

NOTES

1) *Catholic Encyclopedia,* Vol. 7, 1089.

2) *The Official Catholic Directory* (1950) ff.

3) ibid., Statistics.

4) *Catholic Encyclopedia,* Vol. 13, 136.

5) Sister Marie Celeste, S.C., *Elizabeth Ann Seton: A Self-Portrait* (Libertyville, Illinois: Franciscan Marytown Press, 1986).

6) ibid., 261.

7) ibid., 265.

8) *The Official Catholic Directory,* (1996).

9) ibid., (1950 - 1997); cf. *The CARA Report,* Summer 1997 (Washington, D.C.: Georgetown University), Vol. 3, No. 1.

10) Carey, Ann, *Sisters in Crisis,* (Huntington, Indiana: Our Sunday Visitor).

11) Baker, Kenneth,S.J. *Religious Life* (Chicago, Illinois: October 1997), 2.

12) Kelly, George, Book Review, *Religious Life* (Chicago, Illinois: October 1997). Monsignor Kelly lists the names of Sisters and Priests responsible for the religious decline.

13) Sacred Congregation for Religious and for Secular Institutes, "Essential Elements" (Boston: Daughters of St. Paul, May 1983), 23.

14) ibid., 13, 14.

15) ibid., 22.

16) "Instruction on Certain Questions Regarding the Collaboration of the Non-Ordained Faithful in the Sacred Ministry of Priests" (Vatican City: Libreria Editrice Vaticana, 1997) .

17) *The CARA Report,* Summer 1997 (Washington, D.C.: Georgetown University).

Part II

Public School Education in America

CHAPTER 5

Origins and Horace Mann

Some reliable education scholars like to pinpoint the date of the establishment of the first public school in the new land. Others are more cautious about doing so. The truth is that education in the early days of the new nation was made up of a variety of programs and schools, and it is extremely difficult, no matter what one's interest may be, to separate the facts into a clear pattern. Burns and Kohlbrenner wrote an interesting volume in 1937 which they entitled *The History of Catholic Education in the United States.*[1] While their primary objective was to trace out the story of Catholic education at every level in the new land, they also discussed other related matters which indeed helped in forming a picture of how public education began.

These authors point out that three distinct types of schools were prominent in the early years of our country: first, the parochial school (Catholic schools); second, the pauper school (for the education of the poor); third, the compulsory state school.[2]

Education in the colonial and pre-republic period was a patchquilt of school programs. Besides Catholic schools, many other types of parochial schools existed. Many Christian denominations had made their way to the new land and founded their own communities, creating diversity among the schools. It was not only the Catholics who initiated parochial schools but there were many others including the Quakers, Lutherans, Moravians, Mennonites, Baptists, Dunkers, and several others which felt compelled to teach their own children the basic skills and, of course, their own religious beliefs.[3]

There were also, as Burns and Kohlbrenner point out, the pauper schools. These were for children who had no particular religious affiliation and needed educational help. The first pauper schools were often conducted by Catholics, and sometimes by other religious groups, or civic organizations.

Virginia had a strict state parochial system, dominated and controlled by the State established religion, Episcopalianism.[4]

So the picture of education in the early days of this new nation was anything but clear. McClusky notes three main patterns of education:[5] the Northern and Southern Colonies' schools stood in great contrast to those developed in the Middle Colonies. In the North there was great interest in developing laws which would help to bring about an adequate school program. McClusky writes about "the old Deluder Act of 1647."[6] That Act was an effort to keep Satan in his place by requiring that in every "township with 50 householders" a teacher be appointed and a school provided. The law provided that parents of the pupils pay the bill.

In the Southern Colonies, McClusky tells us, religious influence was significant in the schools because the established church of the area was the Angelican Church. Thus the Angelican clergy had complete control over the schools, and it was their responsibility to check on the school masters and be sure that they were good men and had religious opinions acceptable to the Church of England.[7]

McClusky's third pattern of school development was best typified by Pennsylvania.[8] The Quaker Colony had a reputation in those early days as a likable and friendly place to settle and Pennsylvania was particularly known for accepting churches and schools of various denominations. Burns and Kohlbrenner list the takers as "the Quakers, Lutherans, Moravians, Mennonites, Dunkers and others."[9] McClusky in his list adds the Presbyterians and the Baptists and ends with "...and even Catholics." He also notes that the status in New York and New Jersey approximated that of Pennsylvania.[10]

So there were several patterns of education, according to those who have studied that period of our history, and these yielded a multiplicity of different schools. All of them bring out clearly that the control of education in those days was ecclesiastical rather than civil.

The question foremost in the minds of the early leaders of the country was how could every child be assured a good education even when the child lacked religious affiliation, or family, or other interest in education. A number of events occurred which made an answer possible.

No formal relationship existed among the state, the church, the parochial schools, the pauper schools, and the church-established schools. Each had its own arrangement in so far as the content taught and the students accepted. There was no higher authority to organize these various schools or to keep them in line. As McClusky points out, and indeed Burns and Kohlbrenner also note, the educational programs in those early days were under the direction of the church and not of the civil authority.[11] Clearly the civil authority took a second place to religion even in the Thirteen Colonies, nine of which had established religions. Because Church authority was primary, the school system created an amazing mosaic — all the pieces were there but they were not in any particular order.

Perhaps the first step toward reaching a practical solution occurred in New Hampshire. O'Neil presents several tables which summarize interesting legal aspects of this problem.[12] The first table shows "First state action forbidding sectarian instruction in schools," and the second table is entitled, "First state action forbidding public funds to denominational schools." New Hampshire, one of the original Thirteen Colonies admitted to the Union in 1788 as the ninth state, was the first to enact a statute forbidding any funds for denominational schools, except, of course, their own. When the Colony broke away from the English rule, it retained its Protestant aspect. The new state constitution (1784) still showed its prejudice against Catholics. A religious test that excluded Catholics from major offices in the state was retained. However, their new Constitution (Article 6) authorized towns to support public Protestant teachers of piety, religion, and morality.

Few Catholics took up residence in New Hampshire but when the immigration of 1840 occurred the situation changed. Catholics who arrived in New Hampshire found their presence to be resented especially by the active group known as the Know-Nothings. In 1855 this group elected as governor Ralph Metcalf, whose greatest claim to fame was his anti-Catholic talk given to the Legislature at his installation.

Even though New Hampshire passed its law forbidding funds to denominational schools in 1792, sectarian instruction in public schools was not forbidden. But before the end of the nineteenth century, every state in the Union had a section in its Constitution prohibiting the establishment of religion. All but two, McClusky tells us, prohibited either the teaching of religion or the support of religious schools. These were severe blows to all religious education and especially to Catholics.

McClusky points out what he calls a celebrated caricature of the Pope in the New England Primer.[13] The artist depicted a towering ugly figure whose head was crowned with a tiara. Lines designated by letters radiated from different parts of the body. On the opposite page children could find an explanation of the diagram. (Do not be distracted by the old English spelling.)

Advice to Children
Child, behold that man of sin, the Pope, worthy of thy utmost hatred.
Thou shall find in his head, (A) heresy
In his shoulders (B) the supporters of disorder
In his heart (C) mallace, murder and treachery
In his arms (D) cruelity
In his knees (E) false worship and idolatry
In his stomach (F) insatiable covetousness
In his Lyons (G) the worst of lust

The picture is not a pretty one. Such caricatures indicate the level of anti-Catholicism in the northern colonies of early America. The happiness, the justice, and the peace which the new nation promised immigrants was not for the Catholics. When the bishops met at Baltimore in 1829 in solemn council they expressed their deep concern about such educational problems in these words: "We judge it absolutely necessary that schools be established in which the young may be taught the principles of faith and morality while being instructed in letters."[14]

That same Council issued a warning about the use of textbooks that were beginning to dominate the schools and were found to be steeped in anti-Catholicism.

It had to be evident to even the casual observer of the situation that there was a terrible relationship between Catholics and the other citizens of the new country. Anti-Catholicism in the new land was summarized briefly in Chapter I. Here one should note that efforts were made, not only to recognize these facts, but to try to do something about them. Throughout the nineteenth century, as already noted, Catholics made positive efforts to remedy a difficult situation. One thing they would not do was to give up their schools. Catholic schools were the greenhouse of the next generation of Catholics. Indeed this was the way young Catholics were prepared for active and full membership in the Church. Everything had to be done to maintain Catholic schools.

The laws of the Colonies and subsequent States were discouraging to Catholics. It is clear from the laws passed that there was not even the remotest intention to offer any support to the parents of Catholic parochial school students. The exclusion of Catholic schools was evident from the beginning of the new nation. Dunn records an interesting event which occurred in Philadelphia near the end of 1853. A teacher threatened all pupils to read the Protestant Bible or to be expelled. The parish priest, Father John Bapst, S.J. noted that the school committee stated that they were determined to protestantize the Catholic children.[15]

Despite such terrible situations, Catholic authorities made other approaches to state educators and local civil authorities in an attempt to solve this crisis. Several compromise plans were developed in the early years. (cf. Chapter I) The Lowell Plan[16] was one that had temporary success and was developed in Massachusetts in the town of the same name, from 1831 to 1852. Both the public school and Catholic school population seemed sympathetic to this effort. The Lowell plan brought together the Irish Catholics (as Burns and Kohlbrenner identify them) and the other children of the district into a recently built public school. The terms of this arrangement were: 1) The instructors must be examined as to their qualifications by the committee and receive their appointments from them. 2) The books, exercises and studies must be prescribed and regulated by the committee and no other whatever must be taught or allowed. 3) These schools must be placed as respects the examination, inspection and general supervision of the committee on precisely the same footing as the other schools of the town.[17]

The negotiations were represented on the Catholic side by a Father Conelly who insisted that the instructors must be of the Catholic faith and that the books prescribed should contain no statements unacceptable to Catholics. Interestingly enough there was nothing stated in the agreement about religious instruction.

Burns and Kohlbrenner again point out that the religious instruction was almost a certainty because Bishop Benedict Fenwick of the local see was known to be very firm on Catholic religious instructions. Unfortunately the program had mixed results and was terminated in 1852. In that same year the Catholics established their own school in Lowell under the direction of the Notre Dame Sisters.

Other factors contributed to the development of the common school system in the first part of the nineteenth century: the belief that religious teaching is essential in education and the idea of a "Common School." No one accepted the idea that there could be education at the elementary or the secondary level without religion in the curriculum. The importance of religion in education was an accepted theory by most of the people of the new world. Hence there was no argument about whether there would be religious instruction. The question that had to be solved was whose religion should be given in the schools: the Protestant, the Episcopalian, the Baptist, the Presbyterian. The sad part of this very important objective was that in deciding about forming a public institution available to all children absolutely no consideration was given in this phase of the debate to any role to be played by the Catholic religion.

In New York City, DeWitt Clinton was one of the leaders in promoting the idea of a Common School. Such a school would enroll all students despite their diversity. When he became the Governor of New York State he had greater influence in bringing this matter before a wider audience and he gladly used his influence to do so.

One of the most outstanding parishes in New York City at that time was St. Peter's, which regularly appealed for funds to the Free School Society. This group was founded for the education of poor children who did not belong to any religious organization. Burns and Kohlbrenner tell in great part the interesting story of this Free School Society,[18] which soon changed its name to the Public School Society. Considered one of the great philanthropic groups in existence at that time, it supported pleasant and acceptable relations with its member organizations including Catholic schools. But interference in 1840, by Governor Seward and Dr. Nott, President of the Union College, caused the alienation of many religious groups in the City. The schools which they supported became so blatantly and so offensively Protestant that many religious groups refused to patronize them.

At this point Bishop John Hughes entered the controversy claiming from the Society financial support for eight Catholic schools with an enrollment of 3,000 youngsters. Bishop Hughes wrote a brilliant letter petitioning for this help.[19] The Bishop claimed support on the basis of the civic purposes of these Catholic schools. After all these schools achieved the same purposes as the public schools in so far as civic objectives were concerned. But Bishop Hughes added that the Catholic schools also "taught principles of morality calculated to be of great value to society."

Bishop John Hughes wrote a second letter on the same subject to the City Council. The bishop made giant concessions to the civil authorities but he refused to budge on the Catholic position on religion in the schools. When the matter was voted on by the City Council, the proposal received only one vote. Because of a terrible debate which took place before the Council meeting, the resolution was overwhelmingly defeated.

When the issue of teaching religion was brought to the State Legislature, political factions and fear of "Popery" aroused tempers to the point that no solution could emerge.

The final stage in the development of a common or public school system was the appointment of Horace Mann as the Secretary of the State School Board in Massachusetts. His role in this entire effort was the key to the establishment of what eventually would be the Public School System.

HORACE MANN (1796-1859)

Horace Mann was born on a farm in Franklin, Massachusetts in 1796. Of Puritan background, he himself speaks of his association with the Calvinist Religion.

Not much is known about Mann's early education, although we are told by Dunn that he had to be tutored in Latin in order to gain admission to Brown University in 1860. It was there that Mann became enamored with the humanistic philosophy of John Locke. We are told that he also had an enthusiasm for Phrenology. Both the Humanism of Locke and Phrenology were forms of Deism. Adapting Christianity to the new age of reason and science was the aim of both of these philosophies.

Educated as an attorney, Mann was elected to the State Legislature until his 1837 resignation to take on the position of Secretary of the State School Board of Massachusetts. Here he renewed his efforts to establish a common school system in his State, earning him the title of "Father of the Common School."

As Secretary of the State School Board Mann was in an ideal position to influence the development of the local State system and therefore to influence the development of the American educational system. His common school became the predecessor of the modern public school in America. It was a school for everyone: the rich, the poor, the intelligent, the ignorant; all children, regardless of religious background or parental choice, would be educated together.

It was clear to Mann that an educated citizenry would be absolutely essential if the Government of the people was to survive. He, therefore, designed a program intended to meet the educational needs of all. But Mann was a creature of his age, an age in which religion played an important role. Early in his career Horace Mann believed that there should be room in his educational program for a general Protestant religious instruction, but as his idea of the Common School developed, he came to the conclusion that the battle was not only against Catholicism, which he rejected outright, but with all sectarian religions. Mann had a clear anti-Catholic bias which, according to Dunn[20], was "based...on certain errors of fact." Dunn tells us that Mann speaks of "that Vice-Gerent of Hell, the Pope of Rome" who he believed forgave sins in return for the payment of money and granted permission for further sin if more money was forthcoming.[21] Dunn, who did a scholarly study of this period of American history tells us that Horace Mann was actually a deeply religious person but he did not accept the supernatural or, as Dunn states, "it never became vital to him."[22] He seemed to have a conviction that religion of some sort must form a part of every true education and should therefore find a place in his Common School curriculum.[23]

He accepted certain religious and moral principles: the Protestant Bible was, of course, the favorite; the Protestant "Our Father"; the Protestant principle of private interpretation; and the example of Jesus Christ. Dunn also mentions in his study that Mann wanted to include "the fundamental principles of Christianity."[24] McClusky states that "Christianity for Mann was the Christianity of the Ten Commandments, the Golden Rule, the Beatitudes, the example of Christ and other biblical characters, — in sum, the moral and ethical aspects of the religion revealed in the Bible."[25]

When the position of Secretary of Education was offered to Mann he had difficult and conflicting emotions concerning his ideals and his fear of pride and self-serving. Dunn quotes a passage from Mann's diary written on the very day that the position of Secretary was offered to him: "God grant me an annihilation of selfishness, a mind of wisdom, a heart of benevolence! How many men I shall meet who are accessible only through a single motive, or who are incased in prejudice and jealousy, and need, not to be subdued, but they need be remodeled!…There is but one spirit in which these impediments can be met with success: it is the spirit of self-abandonment, the spirit of martyrdom…. In all this, there must be a higher object than to win personal esteem, or favor, or worldly applause. A new fountain may now be opened. Let me strive to direct its current in such a manner that if, when I have departed from life, I may still be permitted to witness its course, I may behold it broadening and deepening in an everlasting progression of virtue and happiness."[26]

Mann's personal convictions about religion were never reflected in the Common School which he instituted. There was, however, a watered-down version of Protestantism in his philosophy of education, but he opposed vigorously all sectarianism in the Common School.[27] This was indeed also difficult for the Protestant sects to accept, as they struggled against Mann for a long period of time with the issue of how much religion could be included in the Common School curriculum.

Although Horace Mann began life as a Calvinist, his religious affiliation changed as he grew older. Near the end of his life he became a Unitarian. Dunn writes that Mann was a "believer in the immortality of the soul" and therefore "education should prepare for the life to come."[28] While he had a special bias against the Catholic religion, Mann's greatest conflict came with his fellow Protestants whose sectarianism he would not tolerate in the Common School Curriculum.

Those who have done critical studies of his work refer to Horace Mann as essentially a rationalist and certainly a budding naturalist. O'Connell maintains that despite his religious reputation and propensities, science and the scientific method dominated his thinking. For that reason Mann stressed the use of science and physiology in all of education, and maintained that if a person really understood nature, all difficulties in life would disappear.[29]

Most scholars believed that the main contribution of Horace Mann was to move the American stage away from the universally accepted religious involvement and place it on the trail of pure naturalism and secularism. This he did almost by default. Many scholars maintain that the right of conscience was carefully protected by Mann for those who objected to traditional Protestant indoctrination. They like to point to the 1827 law which is often referred to as the beginning of a legal tradition of freedom of religion in education. This law was the first in a series of such enacted at the State level. Dunn puts the entire matter in this sentence: "It did not set itself in opposition to the American social tradition that 'religion belongs.' It said rather the rights of conscience must be respected."[30] But the rights of conscience were not protected for those, and there were many, who considered Mann's version of Protestantism as simply another sectarian system.

Dunn finishes his intense study of Horace Mann by giving a picture of the educational situation in Massachusetts in 1848.[31] It was that year that Mann resigned and was elected to the United States Congress, where he served until 1852.

"1) While the legal separation of Church and State ended in Massachusetts (and the nation) with the disestablishment of the Congregational Church in 1833, the social tradition of the union of religion in public life and the essential place of religion in public education remained.

"2) The teaching of doctrinal religion which had been accepted as a part of public education was legally restricted and in practice was gone or almost completely gone.

"3) The religious teaching which remained, speaking only of that which enjoyed official sanction, was composed of ethics, natural theology, and what was gotten from reading of the Bible.

"4) The rights of conscience were protected for those who objected to traditional Protestant indoctrination (with the exception of those who considered straight Bible reading without the authoritative interpretation of their Church as a sectarian tenet in itself).

"5) The rights of conscience were not protected for those who considered Mann's ideas on religion a sectarian system."

Dunn fails to mention that Catholicism was excluded from any sort of partnership in American education by Mann's program.

Horace Mann died on August 2, 1859 in Yellow Springs, Ohio.

NOTES

1) Burns, J.A. and Kohlbrenner, B.J.,*The History of Catholic Education in the United States* (New York: Benzinger Bros., 1937).

2) ibid, 42.

3) ibid, 42.

4) ibid, 42.

5) McClusky, Neil G., S.J., *Catholic Viewpoint on Education* (New York: Image Books, 1962), 2-4.

6) ibid, 2.

7) ibid, 3.

8) ibid, 4.

9) Burns and Kohlbrenner, p. 42.

10) McClusky, 5.

11) ibid., 3, cf. Burns and Kohlbrenner, 43.

12) O'Neil, J. M., *Religion and Education Under the Constitution* (New York.Harper and Bros., 1949), 141.

13) McClusky, 11, cf. Dunn, 264 ff.

14) *Catholic Encyclopedia,* Vol. 2, 40.

15) Dunn, 273.

16) Burns and Kohlbrenner, 156 ff., cf. McClusky, 18, 19, 20.

17) Burns and Kohlbrenner, 157.

18) ibid., 70.

19) ibid., 159.

20) Dunn, William K., *What Happened to Religious Education* (Baltimore: John Hopkins Press, 1958), 137.

21) ibid., 125 n. 24.

22) ibid. 127.

Judged from his writing and actions, Horace Mann comes out a Theist; he comes out a Unitarian in his overt rejection of the Orthodox teachings; and he comes out something of a Deist (despite all of his talk of God as a Father) in his belief in a

God who made the world and then left it pretty much to itself until it should turn at least its human inhabitants back to Him for judgment.

23) ibid., 135.

24) ibid. 137.

25) McClusky, 9.

26) Dunn, 123.

27) ibid., 139.

28) ibid., 137.

29) O'Connell, Jeffrey, *Naturalism in American Education* (New York: Benzinger Bros., 1938), 73-74.

30) Dunn, 182-183.

31 ibid., 187.

CHAPTER 6

John Dewey (1859-1952) and Public Education

Horace Mann played a key position in the development of public education in the United States. Although Mann's contribution is unknown and unappreciated by many, as a matter of fact, it was a most significant one. Horace Mann was responsible in great part for the development of the Common School. In the process of achieving this he made clear that education should have religion in its curriculum. A school without religion, Mann insisted, would be a disaster. Despite his regard for religious education, Mann made it equally clear that there was no room for the Catholic religion. His problem, therefore, was principally a conflict with eight or nine other vocal religious groups who thought that their version of Protestantism should be chosen for the Common School. But Mann turned the tables on all of them and created his own version of religion.

When Mann died in 1859, two important things took place that would influence his work. First, in Burlington, Vermont, John Dewey was born. That same year Darwin published his famous *Origin of Species*, which announced his evolutionary theory and which promised to give naturalism an even greater significance in the world of science and, of course, public education.

The convergence of these three events was a symbolic assurance at least that naturalism in American life and thought would develop and remain strong. Horace Mann did not found naturalism. Despite his great religious propensities and his deep attachment to religion, especially for youth, Horace Mann paved the way for something to underpin the Common School concept which would exclude Supernaturalism, which he never understood and never promoted. John Dewey did not create naturalism, but he became one of its greatest proponents. As Vincent Edward Smith put it so clearly, "...the achievement of Dewey (was) to have put this thought into emphatic and popular forms harmonizing its various elements, using history and philosophy and the empirical disciplines for support, repeating and developing his message in a prodigious literary output, and influencing the group that in turn makes a profession of influencing, namely, American teachers."[1]

Dewey, a brilliant student, graduated from the University of Vermont with an enviable academic record, taught high school for several years and then, we are told, he enrolled in John Hopkins University, where many early friendships, especially with other professors, would affect his entire life. From John Hopkins, Dewey went to the

University of Michigan in 1884. Ten years later, in 1894, he joined the faculty of philosophy and pedagogy at the University of Chicago. In 1905, eleven years later, he made his way to Columbia University and to the Teachers College, where he continued his double interest — education and philosophy. He stayed here as Professor Emeritus even after his resignation. John Dewey died in 1952.

O'Connell, in his famous study of naturalism in American education, defines naturalism as "the attitude of mind characteristic of all systems of thought which deny the existence of an order transcending nature and sense-experience and confine the explanation of reality to the general viewpoint that nature contains the normal and only final answer to all philosophical problems."[2] Naturalism in other words traces its origin back to the Greek philosopher Heraclitus whose favorite slogan was "everything is change." Darwin pointed out that nature was not only the home of man but also his birth place.[3] Man is a product of nature, his problems come from nature, his solutions are found in nature, he obeys the laws of nature, he struggles for his existence against nature, and finally when he dies he goes down to sleep in his natural home.[4] What Dewey accomplished in his naturalistic philosophy was enhanced by the superimposition of what Smith calls "the New Dynamism of Darwinian Evolution."[5]

Dewey is famous for an article he wrote in 1944 and which was edited by a man named Krykorian[6] in which he presented fifteen essays penned by great thinkers in the country (*Naturalism and the Human Spirit*, 1944). Dewey devoted the entire article to denouncing supernaturalism. Unless something could be empirically tested, he insisted, it did not exist and should not be considered as a proper subject for philosophy.

Vincent Smith, a brilliant scientist and philosopher, indicates that Dewey had three aspects to his philosophy by which he enriched his life to the study and keeping of the "continuum of nature by using the empirical method." This process would be accomplished in a person's socio-cultural environment. Smith suggests that such a concept of Dewey's philosophy then, could be understood under three headings: the world and man; b) what man should do; c) the instrument for man. Man, naturalism tells us, is simply a new pattern of matter. Experience is merely the interaction between the organism (for example, man) and his environment. The mind is just another form of matter and, not surprisingly, thinking is the very same thing, that is, another form of matter.

Dewey's roots as a naturalist came from his study of biology. Smith points out that some evolutionists leave the biological level when they get to man because they consider psychological activity of mind as a new and meta-biological dimension. Dewey never gets this far. All his aims, Smith tells us, are social, and he achieves neither absolute beginnings nor does he find ultimate ends. Man lives in a continuum — a continuum of material. Smith tells us that Dewey hints that thought is simply some kind of vocal speech where the thinker is talking to himself.

Chapter 6 – John Dewey (1859-1952) and Public Education

The second division Dewey reflects on is "What man should do." In other words, what are his goals or "his moralism"? Dewey is deeply immersed in social values. He feels that his pragmatism should close the gap between man's triumph in the empirical disciplines and his social and cultural progress. However, he makes it clear that his proposals are different from those given by Aristotle and the Scholastics in this same area. There are, according to Dewey, "no fixed ends." If an end is achieved it is not permanent nor unchangeable because it is always changing and therefore moving toward something else. Ends in a true sense are nothing more than means to further goals, and as Smith points out, "...if such a premise be admitted, then ends perish and means monopolize reality." What man has to do is to try to keep up with the ever-evolving world.

Smith tells us that Dewey speaks for man's striving for "fulfillment," but, says Smith, it is difficult to see "just what is being fulfilled except what is called organic needs." The continuum chosen by Dewey is neither beginning nor end to its ongoing character. Dewey cannot point out any true future or universal ends. His concern is about consequences and indeed immediate consequence, rather than about ultimates and absolutes. Dewey's judgments may never be called absolute, and his method of valuing in terms of consequences he labels *instrumentalism*.

According to Dewey, things are good, valuable, only in terms of the consequences which they bring. He never considers the intrinsic nature of realities. Smith goes on to say that "...man is briefed to view as good or bad whatever may or may not have propitious consequences in adapting him better to his social and cultural changes."

Dewey never defines thinking or thought. For John Dewey man is not primarily a thinker, but a tool-making, too-using, tool-intoxicating animal.

The third vision that Smith suggests for understanding Dewey's philosophy is to be found in the part entitled "The Instrument for Man." Dewey's logic has often been called a theory of inquiry. It is a process of continuing questioning. Smith reminds us that Dewey does not present an account of how we ought to think but merely describes a way of thinking. Man therefore simply continues his process of inquiry and testing within the continuum of nature, going from one material thing to another.

Man tries to solve his problems when he collects data, checks it out operationally through experience, and discovers its consequences. If its consequences do not work, or they fail to solve his problem, they are scrapped..

Smith also points out that knowledge in Dewey is relative. He is not interested in truth as a goal, thus crumbling another noble achievement of Aristotle. Inquiry is the important effort to be made: a natural event like eating and sleeping where mind is simply physico-chemical energies transformed into more subtle patterns.

For Dewey there are no absolutes, unchanging truths, except for that of inquiry. For Dewey and his naturalistic colleagues there could not be an approach to reality *except* through empirical methods. What Dewey has done is to reduce man's activities to that of *making*.

Like Smith, O'Connell[7] also analyzes the philosophy of John Dewey. Smith is a scientist and philosopher. His approach to John Dewey had advantages over that of O'Connell who was an educator and a philosopher. Both scholars surprisingly arrived at similar, sometimes identical conclusions.

O'Connell admits that John Dewey was one of the great minds in nineteenth century America. As a philosopher and as a teacher Dewey established an outstanding record of educational writings, living to see naturalistic philosophy accepted in almost every American public institution.

In his youth he had embraced a Hegelian philosophy, but he soon abandoned this idealism for a more pragmatic philosophy of education which has merited the label "Instrumentalism." Practically speaking, this means that there were no absolute purposes or goals in Dewey's idea of education. Only what had proved effective in repeated experimentation could be considered good. Science, then, is the instrument perfectly suited to test the value of any goals. The final test was "whatever works" is true, right, and good.[8]

When we say that John Dewey is a naturalist we mean that to him nature explains all things; no order transcends it. Dewey studied many thinkers, but is indebted especially to Darwin's development of evolution. According to his thinking, appealing to absolutes of any sort (such as God) is nonsense. Soul, mind, reason, intelligence, and such ideas once so popular, and which came to us from the past, are now meaningless. These represent a level beyond the natural and such entities are not created by God (there is no God); they are created by man's mind.[9]

While Dewey has some kind words for some of the things which religion accomplished in the past, he warns us that religious belief is imply a waste of time. We must keep in mind that Dewey did not believe in God; he rejects the very important ideas of revelation and the supernatural; he holds that God is but a projection of man's ideals. His definition makes us think of Freud's concept of God, for he also maintained that God was a creation of man's mind.

Science, especially with the help of Darwin, explains totally through Evolutionism the origin of everything, including man. Naturalists did not believe that there were any important commandments or laws. Such precepts were obsolete and useless and the result of superstition. Hence, Dewey rejected the concept of an eternally fixed moral law.[10] He also rejected the teaching that man participated in and could know, through the natural law, the eternal law of God. The moral laws were formed and developed by men and therefore could be changed as men thought best. The real moral laws of men were only those of nature and the concerns of society.

Dewey's philosophy of life became his philosophy of education. Both are, of course, naturalistic.[11] Consequently his educational theory ignored God, the supernatural level, the soul, immortality, and any moral law which was beyond the level of nature or society. Education is for the present. A child is educated for childhood; a youth is educated to be a youngster; and an older person does not need any goals or ends, for these are developed as he grows older and as he needs them. Children must learn the proper instrument and proper tests, which are "whatever works."

Catholics object to Dewey's philosophy principally because he excludes every spiritual dimension of life. It is easy to understand why religion is not needed in his curriculum. His rejection of teleology denies any purpose for man beyond this life. Finally, instrumentalism excludes all worry about good and evil, for instrumentalism makes what works the good and what fails the evil.

John Dewey lived until 1952. From 1904 to 1930, after successful assignments at the Universities of Michigan, Minnesota, and Chicago, he became a professor at the famous Columbia University in New York. He was considered the most prominent spokesperson for the Progressive Movement in education, and his principles and theories were translated into action by the most prominent educators in the country: particularly by noted presidents of prestigious colleges and, of course, by his own disciples.

It will be helpful to examine one aspect of Dewey's philosophy of life so that we can compare it with the Catholic version of the same: Supernaturalism is the philosophy of St. Thomas Aquinas and his disciples.

Since religion was no longer permitted in the public school, many leading educators have suggested that ethics might be a good substitute and urge that ethics be included in the curriculum. Does it — can it — substitute for religion in the curriculum?

DEWEY'S ETHICS:
John Dewey wrote one of his earlier books on *A Critical Theory of Ethics*.[12] He was then a professor at the University of Michigan and was a young man of approximately 33 years. Published by the Greenwood Press in New York, the book was re-printed in 1957 by another publishing house. In the meantime, Dewey had many other things to say about public education and ethics, and even published another work on the same subject in 1922.

Ethics according to Dewey is the science of conduct.[13] He clearly maintains in the opening discussion of ethics that the agent operates by aim or purpose. In fact he insists that there can only be conduct when one has a purpose for an action. Such a being is a moral agent in his actions, and his actions, when conscious, are conduct.[14] Aware that the end of the action is important, Dewey writes: "Since it is the end which gives action its moral value, what is the true end, summum bonum, of man…the question of rightness of conduct is simply a special form of the question concerning the nature of the end or good…the end or good decides what should be or ought to be."[15] Holding that the moral agent is capable of right or wrong, Dewey continues to search for the goal which explains all this. After a lengthy discussion of some hundred pages he writes: "The ethical postulate, the pre-supposition involved in conduct, is this: IN THE REALIZATION OF INDIVIDUALITY THERE IS

FOUND ALSO THE NEEDED REALIZATION OF SOME COMMUNITY OF PERSONS OF WHICH THE INDIVDUAL IS A MEMBER, AND CONVERSELY, THE AGENT WHO DULY SATISFIES THE COMMUNITY IN WHICH HE SHARES, BY THAT SAME CONDUCT SATISFIES HIMSELF."[16]

Dewey spent his lifetime trying to clear up misunderstandings of his ideals.

There are three aspects to Dewey's ethics. An ethical act must be 1) an experience which is not merely private, 2) but also public, and 3) it must be an experience which satisfies the agent and society. It enables an individual to achieve the end chosen; a valid judgment cannot be ordered to the satisfaction of one's immediate or selfish desire. The standard is rather the well being of both ourselves and also other members of our society.[17] Social aims dominate Dewey's philosophy.

One of Dewey's followers wrote an essay for the National Society for the Study of Education Yearbook in 1981. Clive M. Beck[18] of the Ontario Institute for Studies in Education writes: "...the question of what is right is always complex and is always open...one's undestanding of what is right or valuable constantly grows and hence changes."[19] Dewey's approach to the question of truth and to all moral matters is open-ended. Dewey points out that education itself is a continual reconstruction and reorganization of experiences. Such reconstruction, he maintains, continually adds meaning and increases the ability to direct the course of subsequent experiences. Dewey's concept of right and wrong has sometimes been described as "whatever works is right and should be done, and whatever does not work is wrong and, therefore, should be avoided." Dewey clearly has a final purpose to his philosophy: the social good.[20] Whatever improves society is good, whatever does not improve society is bad. The entire end or goal, the summum bonum of his philosophizing is the social or common good, the betterment of society or democracy. And since society is aiming toward the ideal, evolving is a constant process of growth and change; its goal cannot be attained.

Dewey rejects absolute ends, finding "endless ends" in every situation. Thus the question of good and evil becomes simple in pragmatism or instrumentalism. The standard is the well being of both the individual and the other members of society. Hence his emphasis is on the achievement of the social or the common good as a final(?) end or purpose. Brubacher, a disciple of Dewey, refers to this "goal" as "sharing in democracy." And since there are no real ends, democracy simply leads to more democracy or more sharing of democracy.[21]

Again a good realized by the will of one individual has a public effect. Practical common good makes the moral order of society,[22] and constitutes the "purpose" of Dewey's ethics.

Dewey's position on absolutes is revealed in these words: "There has been much useless discussion as to the absolute or relative character of morals...if absolute means immobile and rigid, it is anything but desirable that morals should be absolute." And he further explains: "If the physical world is a scene of movement in which there is no rest it is a poor compliment to pay the moral to conceive it as static and lifeless. A rigid criterion in a world of developing social relations would speedily prove no criterion at all."[23]

Dewey is convinced that the whole purpose of life as expressed in his works on ethics is to achieve a perfect, growing, ideal society. This is clearly a form of socialism. Since such is not possible, he settles for what he speaks of as an improved, growing and ever changing society. Dewey is the new Heraclitus because everything is constantly changing.[24]

ST. THOMAS AQUINAS

St. Thomas lived from 1224 until 1274.[25] He was one of the most influential theologians and philosophers in the long history of the Catholic Church. The Church has in fact named Thomas Aquinas the patron of Catholic schools. A brilliant young man, who would only live to his 50th year, created incredible work in developing a philosophy and theology still widely used throughout the Church as its official program.

St. Thomas called ethics a philosophical study of voluntary human actions with the purpose of determining what type of activities are good, right, and to be done, or bad, wrong, and not to be done, so that man could live well.[26] His chief concern was to discover which of man's actions should be done and which ones should be avoided.

Concerned only with voluntary human actions, which are under the direction of the intellect and the will, Thomas' ethics attempts to discover a well-considered reflective and reasonable set of conclusions concerning those voluntary actions which may be considered good or evil. St. Thomas wishes to bring "…rational order into the domain of man's own voluntary acts."

In St. Thomas' formal consideration of ethics he presents the subject under two headings: Individual Ethics (voluntary actions as they are related to the private good of the individual), and Social Ethics (as they are related to the common good.)[27] Every moral person must use his intellect and will in order to bring about a rational ordering of his life. Thomism teaches that good actions earn moral credit or merit and that evil actions gain sanctions. It also notes that all individuals have the same specific purpose or end, not only personal good and satisfaction but also social satisfaction. Persons seek some being great enough to be an inexhaustible object of human knowing and loving. That being is God. Therefore, all human actions that bring man closer to an understanding and to the love of God are good; actions that remove one from that fulfillment are evil.[28]

There is then a marked difference between Thomism or Supernaturalism, the official Catholic understanding of ethics, and the teaching of John Dewey. In John Dewey there is first the personal satisfaction of the individual by his purposive actions, and the common good or the improvement of the social good.[29] This is what we might call the summum bonum for John Dewey, although he would not use that term because it does not seem possible for anyone to achieve such an end. Dewey's response to a final end is simply that inquiry into life is open-ended. There is really no summum bonum. The social end is as far as one can go; it is continued growth in democracy. Catholic philosophy goes a long step further — the summum bonum is God. Human acts that lead to God are good; those leading away from God are evil.[30]

Purely philosophical ethics cannot achieve the ultimate purpose St. Thomas seeks. "As sacred doctrine is based on the light of faith so is philosophy founded on the natural life of reason."[31] Nevertheless, reason can achieve remarkable goals in the natural area.

Reason brings St. Thomas into the realm of the natural moral law. In this area he begins all his judgments about good and evil with an absolute principle: "good is to be done and sought after; evil is to be avoided."[32] But Thomas contends that using reason alone cannot attain for man his true goal or end which is God, the Summum Bonum. This takes one into the domain of faith.

Thomism deals with the question of natural law, which helps us understand something about absolutes. In the Summa Theologica[33] Thomas treats this subject at length. One of the first questions he faces is whether the natural law is one or many. And he concludes that there are several such precepts; the natural law has many first principles. He refers to certain self-evident principles such as: man is a rational animal; every whole is greater than its parts; things equal to one and the same are equal to one another. He also speaks of certain indemonstrable principles as: the same thing cannot be affirmed and denied at the same time; the notion of being and non-being. The practical reason is identified first, because it is founded on the principle that good is that which all seek. Hence, the first precept of law: good is to be done and pursued and evil is to be avoided.[34]

Actually Thomas' first principles should not worry the pragmatist. What seems to bother them is the issue of morality which involves such absolutes as the Ten Commandments, the law of love, and similar universal binding absolutes. Many scholars maintain that the second part of the Decalogue is part of the natural law which sets certain absolute limits which cannot be violated without detriment to human dignity. Dewey deals with this very subject in his Ethics. (35) In a single paragraph Dewey dismisses the entire subject of absolutes. The Ten Commandments are not a concern of his philosophy, nor even his Ethics.

Aside from murder, the Commandments set clear limitations on such other things as stealing, lying, committing adultery, and the Commandments prohibit the taking of all human life, including the life of the unborn. These are the kind of absolute principles which seem to concern the pragmatist, atheist, or the instrumentalist who rejects them outright.

Two points must be considered. In the reflective approach by Beck, a follower of Dewey and an enemy of the supernatural, these points about Thomistic philosophy are studies. First of all, Beck points out that Dewey's concept of moral inquiry as indicated, is open-ended. The reason that Dewey maintained this is clear. There is nothing absolute to stop the open-ended inquiry. In other words, one never really arrives at a final answer — an additional answer was not only possible but inevitable. Beck writes that "...Dewey was right to reject absolute values and maintained that everything is open; anything may be of value." Interestingly, Beck cautions that in practice "...it is possible and necessary to identify basic human values that persist despite constant reappraisal and that indeed seem to be so much a part of human life that it is difficult to conceive how they could cease to be fundamental to human life."[36] An interesting thought.

The second matter which must be brought to our attention is the question of indoctrination. Beck again reminds us that indoctrination is a huge problem, particularly in moral education. His argument is quite simple and one must acknowledge that it contains much truth. How can we expect young people to be indoctrinated and then grow up to think for themselves? Some of them even indicate that "the pupil" must have the chance to reject any belief either at the time it is presented or in the future. Ever since this was suggested the rejections have been more frequent.

This problem is admittedly a difficult one even for Deweyans. Even Beck is concerned about the many disputes about "whether some degree of inculcation is appropriate in early childhood and whether some moral principles can be taught as established beyond reasonable doubt while others cannot." Schuster, classified as one of the ten eminent public educational leaders, noted that Dewey's proposal was "to bridge the gap between the liberal classroom and his new way of looking at the world, in which Relativism has become the only absolute and so make the past obsolete."

Generally philosophers and theologians make a distinction between teaching *a priori* and *a posteriori*. The former is teaching by proceeding from general principles to individual cases; the latter is proceeding from individual cases to a general principle. *A posteriori*, of course, is acknowledged as the experimental, the scientific, or inductive method in teaching and learning and is acknowledged as an effective way to teach. All good teachers and philosophers would agree. This is the one accepted way of learning or gaining any knowledge, according to Dewey. Remember his method is strictly and exclusively experimental — experimental and inductive. There is no room in his philosophy for the deductive.

The question raised here by Beck, his predecessors and successors, is whether or not teaching or learning or proceeding *a priori* or deductively can be an effective way. Is it a sound teaching and learning method to establish a general principle and then to demonstrate how that principle is to be applied in individual instances? The validity of the *a priori* method, that is, proceeding from the general to the particular, is also a well-established traditional method. It is well known that this method can be used successfully both for children and adults. The *a priori* method is not valid if one does not admit or accept the intellect. If one accepts that the mind can understand, see the relationship between cause and effect, and formulate valid principals and conclusions, then the *a priori* method is indeed valid. Deweyans do not accept this understanding of the intellect nor do they in fact accept any ability or function beyond the material.

A priori deductive method of teaching and learning is valid for both children and adults. Of course, one must accept the mind, reason, ideas, or concepts, or — as Terman puts it — the ability to do abstract thinking. One must learn about the evils of sins to be avoided, not on the street corner — nor by sad individual experience — but by careful teaching and learning of principles which can be applied when needed.

One of the difficulties encountered in discussing these matters in terms of Dewey's pragmatism or his instrumentalism is that Dewey and his disciples do not accept God, or the Commandments, or anything associated with the Supernatural. For example, one does not read in recent secular books of ethics, that Christ taught the universal law of love, a clear absolute which is intended to guide all of us through life. This absolute, namely love God and love your neighbor as you love yourself, is a principle that applies to all people at all times. It admits of no exceptions. But it is, of course, a principle, an ethical principle, revealed by Jesus Christ quoting the Hebrew Testament and by His Father. For this reason it is rejected immediately. In Deweyan philosophy one reads nothing about reason — as a spiritual ability to do abstract thinking, and to draw conclusions and relations between cause and effect. These are merely, for Dewey and his followers, new and different reorganizations or repatterning of matter.

VALUES

One area of ethics which has become popular in recent years among public educators is *value education.*[37] This expression has been popular in modern writings for over a hundred years. There was an effort to make it a distinct branch of philosophy. The concept of value education, popular among Austrian philosophers, was promoted in the United States by John Dewey. This outlook on life begins with the experience of wanting or desiring something — a value or something desirable. The value if good can encourage sound moral activity and behavior and motivate one toward similar goals.

Critics tell us that values fits well into the philosophy of St. Thomas Aquinas because he speaks frequently about the appetite (appetitus.) He described the appetite as "the inclination of a thing arising from its own nature towards something else."[38] That something is the desirable or a value.

John Dewey, because he embraced not only an open-ended inquiry, but also an evolutionary viewpoint, believes that there are no ends. In fact, he is quoted in his book *Human Nature and Conduct* as maintaining that "ends are endless," and again, "there are no ends."[39] Nevertheless, Dewey was responsible for popularizing the concept of values, which are really "ends," and transmitting this to a new generation of modern philosophers.

Some public educators consider value education important enough to be included in the regular curriculum. Beck's article in a 1981 NSSE Yearbook, cited above, deals at length with this subject. He even advises that it would be a good idea to include this subject as a regular part of the educational program. Perhaps this would make a good substitute for religion. At the same time he presents a new approach to value education which he calls a "reflective approach." He writes that "...while all our traditional values — religious, societal, parental — must be open to reflective assessment, each in its turn, one must not regard them as suspect simply because they are traditional."[40] Beck speaks of taking a common set of basic values and lists among them survival, happiness, health, fellowship, helping others, wisdom, fulfillment in life, and so on. One is then to take a basic human value as a reference point, reflect on these and on specific sub-values, and center on value topics or problems in order to motivate certain positive actions or experiences. He points out also that one way to teach these values in the school is to live them. "A school that does not practice what it teaches in the area of values will teach very little."[41] Many value programs have become popular in recent years, but some of those in the Dewey philosophic tradition can be labeled only partial successes. Because of the underlying assumptions of no supernatural level, totally social ends, no ultimates nor absolutes; the limitations are obvious. As one studies these various efforts the expression that lingers on is: "all dressed up and no place to go."

CONCLUSION

St. Thomas Aquinas and his supernatural point of view have been deliberately included in this study of ethics and values. That great philosopher and theologian is normally neglected by modernists since the time of the enlightenment and seldom receives even a footnote in their works. Beck is rather an exception to this rule in this one regard. He mentions in his historical survey of insights from Educational Philosophy that "support for this (moral) view is sometimes derived from Christian teachings, going back in the New Testament itself: 'I do not do the good I would, but the evil I would not is what I do.'" He saves his Deweyan self by asserting this view as overly simplistic even in the view of many Christians.[42] And in another negative reference to capacities and potentialities Beck notes that these latter "after the manner of Aristotle (and Aquinas, in a natural domain) are unworkable." These are typical references to truly relevant and what could be helpful sound Catholic teaching.[43]

It is customary that in reviewing the history of any philosophical question discussed, the Modernists begin with Plato, then go to Aristotle, and then skip over 1600 years to the works of Thomas Hobbes, the great British moral and political philosopher of the modern era. Sometimes they go directly from Aristotle to Descartes and his Dualism. One could meditate on these facts for some time. Isn't there anything that St. Augustine, or the Church's Fathers of the Patristic Period, or St. Thomas and the Scholastics, or hundreds of other great scholars, who together span those nearly seventeen hundred years, could contribute to the growth of human knowledge even when the new attempts are being made by positivists, humanists, pragmatists, instrumentalists and atheists who *a priori* reject the Supernatural, God, and all these stand for? Or is all that effort so tainted by the Supernatural that it now means absolutely nothing? These years — centuries — of course they have labeled the Dark Ages. Nothing good or worthwhile could come from writers in those years. This certainly is a subject for continuing study and consideration. Are the Commandments, the universal Law of Love, the Beatitudes, all those great teachings which are a part of our Judeo-Christian tradition, heritage, and culture to be denied or made light of to ninety percent of the students and adults of America? This decision, made by the Modernists, is one which should be carefully considered by all who have any concern for the education of the youth and the future of this nation.

Chapter 6 – John Dewey (1859-1952) and Public Education

NOTES

1) Smith, Vincent E., *Ideal Men of Today* (Milwaukee: Bruce, 1950), 26.

2) O'Connell, Jeffrey, *Naturalism in American Education* (New York: Benzinger Bros., (1938), 1.

3) Smith, 29 passim.

4) ibid., 29.

5) ibid., 30.

6) ibid., 25 to passim.

7) O'Connell, 104 ff.

8) ibid., 122 ff.

9) ibid.., 114, 118, 119.

10) ibid., 121, 123.

11) ibid., 126 ff.

12) Dewey, John, *Critical Theory of Ethics* (New York: Greenwood Press, 1891 [rev. 1957]).

13) ibid., 1.

14) ibid., 1.

15) ibid., 4.

16) ibid., 131.

17) *Catholic Encyclopedia,* Vol. 5, "Ethics", 577.

18) Beck, Clive; "The Reflective Approach to Values Education," Chapter 8, NSSE Yearbook (1981), 185.

19) ibid., 187

20) O'Connell, 127 ff. "Education in its broadest sense is the means of this social continuity of life." (Democracy and Education) "All values that are not social are rejected."

21) Brubacher, John; *Modern Philosophy* (Hill, 1950), 143.

22) Dewey, 131.

23) ibid., 135.

24) ibid., 138; cf. O'Connell, 242: Socialistic tendencies are very much in evidence in their writings, and while they are not prepared to approve fully the communistic theory of life and education in making the well-being of society, even though it be a democratic one, the sole and exclusive aim of education, they are actually preparing the way for just such a development.

25) *Catholic Encyclopedia,* Vol, 5, "Ethics," 570 ff.

26) ibid., 570.

27) Grett, Josephius, O.S.B., *Elementa Philosophies* (Friburgi Brisgoviae: Herder, 1937), Vol. II, 303 ff.

28) *Catholic Encyclopedia,* Vol. 5, "Ethics," 572.

29) Dewey, 137-138.

30) *Summa Theologica* I – II, (Ottawa, Canada, 1941), 5-8.

31) *Catholic Encyclopedia,* Vol. 5, 57l.

32) *Summa,* 91, 1-4.

33) ibid., 94, 1-6.

34) ibid., 94, 2 passim.

35) Dewey, 203 ff.

36) Beck, 188 to 190 passim.

37) *Catholic Encyclopedia,* Vol. 14, 527 ff.

38) Summa, I-II, 8, 1.

39) Dewey, John, *Human Nature and Conduct* (New York 1922), 229, 232.

40) Beck, 198.

41) ibid., 195.

42) ibid., 191.

43) ibid., 187-203.

CHAPTER 7

Public Education Leaders

The influence of John Dewey and the rejection of supernaturalism along with the exaltation of naturalism won the hearts of many great and influential Americans. These include, of course, the thousands of students of Dewey; some who studied in his classrooms and others who knew him only through his writings, but who carried on his tradition of naturalism. Still others were just "born again" naturalists who did all they could to carry on Dewey's philosophy of godlessness, the demise of supernaturalism, and the exaltation of Naturalism.

CHARLES W. ELIOT (1834 - 1926)[1]
Charles W. Eliot made a significant contribution to the cause of naturalism and the influence it had on American education. An interesting person and educator, who served as President of Harvard University for almost forty years. His stature among his colleagues was most significant; his influence on American education was enormous.

Eliot was a Unitarian who did not believe in Christianity; he did not accept it as a revealed religion. In his writings and lectures he made it clear that there was no such thing, in his way of thinking, as "supernatural" religion. He was committed to nature's law and nothing more. In one of his most revealing lectures, entitled "The Religion of the Future," he made it clear that this was his own personal position on that important subject and he went on to reject any dogma, creed, or institution associated with religion.

Sometimes his philosophy is called a "humanitarian idealism" but his naturalistic "religion" seems to be the basis of everything he accepted and taught. Some critics refer to him as a pragmatist, a definition that fits well his concept of "serviceability."

Eliot, as did all convinced naturalists, excluded any kind of supernatural end or purpose in life either in the present or in the future. Man, using the scientific method, must serve others and thus contribute to the common or social good.

He did not accept an unchanging moral law. Through science, Eliot believed, an individual becomes well trained physically and develops the skills needed for life. He must continue throughout life contacts with the world of man and especially with nature. Service was man's only goal and purpose.

It was individuals of the significant intellectual calibre of Eliot who, preaching from his privileged position at Harvard for forty years, made such an enormous contribution to the development and spread of American naturalism, and the work of Dewey.

WILLIAM KILPATRICK – (1871-1965) (2)

Another important man in this category was William Kilpatrick. A student of John Dewey, he put into practice what Dewey had developed in theory. As a professor and teacher of master teachers, Kilpatrick also added his own touch to American public education.

Kilpatrick was on the faculty of Teachers College, Columbia University, where in 1918 he became Professor of Philosophy of Education. One can hardly question the influence which this man had in the molding of future teachers and especially on the future teachers of American teachers through this privileged position. Philosophically Kilpatrick favored the fact of change. Thus he rejected both the ancient and medieval philosophies of the great thinkers such as Aristotle, Saint Augustine, Saint Thomas. Like his mentor, he also was a devotee of Darwin's work. The origin of species proved that there was nothing unchangeable or spiritual in the traditional sense in all of nature. Nothing in the universe is beyond change for nothing permanent of any kind exists. Like the ancient Heraclitus, Kilpatrick proposed everything changes.

One can immediately understand what the Catholic Church (or any Church) and its teachings meant to Kilpatrick and his followers. The Church believes in and teaches revelation. All its doctrine and dogma are based on the revealed word of God. Kilpatrick and his students held that there was no such thing as revelation, and, when the Church argued for the existence of certain things because of their essential nature, these educators responded that there was no essential nature; there were no absolutes; everything was subject to change.

Obviously Kilpatrick did not accept any of the great truths of religion: God, creation, the soul, immortality, eternal happiness. Man, he believed, is simply subject to the evolutionary process. He must try to improve himself and his society by using the scientific method. Both man's social and economic life are subject to such improvement. Man comes and goes.[3]

According to this belief nothing in this world is unchangeable. Everything must be proven experimentally over and over again, and if it is untested and unproven, it must be rejected. Scientific thinking has freed all of us; the traditional values no longer bind us. We now live in a world that is experimental, pragmatic, and relative, and the only way we can adjust to such a world of change is by testing and experimenting. The outstanding critic, O'Connell, summarizes this matter in the following telling paragraph:

Kilpatrick is perfectly frank in his plea for naturalistic and social morals…his thesis is that of Dewey, only it is more popularly expressed, or easy to understand.

There is no doubt that while his philosophy is experimental naturalism, his religious attitude is atheistic, and consequently his morals and ethics are at most purely social. The only evils that exist are social ones. The only preparation requisite for life is that "for adequate management of social affairs."[4]

JAMES E. McCLELLAN (5)

To get an insight into more current philosophy of education, a brief study into the insights of James E. McClellan will be examined. His article appears in the 80th Yearbook of the National Society for the Study of Education and is entitled "First Philosophy and Education."

In that year (1980-81) McClellan was a Professor of Philosophy and Education at State University in Albany, New York. We can assume that he was considered an outstanding spokesman in this field by his naturalistic colleagues. The Editor of the Yearbook tells us that these basic metaphysical viewpoints represent a contemporary treatment of "First Philosophy" — the search for ultimate reality.

In fact, McClellan begins his article by quoting the eminent philosopher of Education, Theodore Bramele. Philosophy, he writes, "explores the basic sources and aims of life. It asks and tries to answer the deepest questions that man can ask or answer." McClellan begins his work by asking "how to get to the basics." He points out that what he means by First Philosophy is the union of two familiar branches of philosophy — epistemology and ontology, theory of knowledge and theory of being. His work begins with a quotation from Sydney Hook, and the opening lines read as follows: "To encourage philosophers…to derive (the philosophy of education) from some philosophic position such as Idealism, Realism, Thomism, Pragmatism, or Existenialism is to encourage them to perpetuate garrulous absurdities." To see that McClellan accepts Hook's condemnation of these past and present "misuses" of epistemology and metaphysics, these garrulous absurdities, one need only look at a few of the following paragraphs.[6]

In a section entitled "Aristotle finds God,"[7] he concludes as follows:

"Eschewing myths of all the sorts without which Plato could not do philosophy, Aristotle followed the question of motion back to a principle of pure actuality which he called god (Theos)…questioned about the ontology of his prime mover, Aristotle can answer simply: its being, which means being perfect, complete and unchanging, is necessary."

McClellan covers the entire area of First Philosophy from Aristotle to Descartes, which he describes as follows:

"This First Philosphy…is to see the unmoved mover take on the guise of a personal god, to observe the change — one dare not call it progress — in the roles played by Reason, Doubt, Faith, Knowledge in the search of the ultimate cause, to fill the impulse toward surrender to mystical experience and the unconquerable resistance to that impulse, a resistance which gradually came to dominance here where Aristotle's philosophy returns to the West."

So in just a single paragraph McClellan covers all Philosophers to Descartes.[8]

McClellan proposes that: "…the remains from the once majestic Aristotelian-Thomistic Science are long past repairing…Descartes came on the scene with his better design. His mediations on first philosophy were placed before the…most wise and illustrious Deans and Doctors of the sacred faculty of theology in Paris. Unfortunately, and we must agree with him here, they could not support the philosophical and theological claims of the holy Catholic Church. They sensed the revolutionary implications of Decartes' philsophy even if they dared not to refute it."

He points out that Descartes[9] reversed Aristotle; McClellan crushes Descartes in about one and a half pages. He laments Descartes because he says his efforts would not secure "the blessing of the Sacred Faculty of Theology. They knew if he did not, that the method of radical doubt would blow away the tattered remnant of scholasticism." So having disposed of Artistotle and everyone from his time to Descartes' time, McClellan sets about developing a First Philosophy. He writes that one "should recognize that the division between philosophy and science is a recent historical aberration, contemporary with the growth of industrial capitalism, like the latter doomed to either become extinct or else to extinguish us." Philosophy is just another part of materialism for separate study. This is scientism and materialism.

McClellan indicates that when one is trying to develop a First Philosophy it is necessary to stay within the limits of science, and he places the question thus: "Does it include ontological commitments not continuous with physics? If the answer is yes, shall we 'commit it then to the flames?'"[10] What the author is interested in is only a philosophy which like Dewey's is "continuous with physics." If such is not the case he recommends it be dismissed. Like all materialists he insists that things are an object of knowledge only if continuous with physics. His beliefs and commitments do not require ontological commitments beyond physics.

He admits clearly that he is a materialist: "From Democritus to the present the central point of materialism is what I have been calling 'ontological continuity with physics'…Not the content of specific physical theories which varies from one historical epic to another."

"Suppose we ask how this particular animal species happened to invent a science like physics. The materialist wants to understand that process from an evolutionary point of view going back (in principle) to the origin of the universe itself. At that exact moment — more or less — some of the basic matter of the world went evolutionary, evolving over time from the truly elementary particle, whatever they may turn out to be, into sub-atomic particles — electrons... elements (hydrogen, helium, etc.)... then molecules...compounds...organisms...mammal...HomoSapiens...physics. The chain is unbroken. Nothing has been added, nothing taken away."[11]

McClellan ends his paper with a glowing commitment to all that is "continuous with physics."[12]

There is little doubt about what is important to our modern example of public education philosophy. In an article written in the NSSE Yearbook McClellan concluded his contribution with the statement: "One wishes we could return to Thorndike's confidence in the power of a scientific method to give us both the ends and means of education. But we can't."[13] Well, the truth is that McClellan and his colleagues have taken public education a long way back to the great materialists of the past.

This philosophy leaves no space for God, in fact for anything other than the science of Physics; no room for any supernatural or anything associated with it. In the basic philosophy as explained in this document by James McClellan, we find no references to any realities or concepts that Thomists are so familiar with in our daily life and which have been developed by great thinkers and great philosophers over the ages. True, this is only a small part of a total explanation of McClellan's philosophy, but it is enough to let us know that physics is the major concern, the basic and only reality in this philosophy. McClellan is a materialist and naturalist.

MORE LEADERS

In 1971 the National Society for the Study of Education published a two-part Yearbook, the second volume of which was "Leaders in American Education."[14] A panel of twenty-five well-known educators was chosen to make these choices. Admittedly, the Editor notes, there are many other educational leaders, even some chosen by the panel, who were not treated in this volume.

The purpose for this conclusion is to acknowledge that the five educators selected for this study and examined briefly above in no way exhaust the leadership in American education. They were selected because, in a sense, they represented certain ideational departures in the development of the Common School, or because they appeared in different historical periods and by their position in time and the impact of their thought made a contribution to new growth in American education and certainly to its philosophy.

Horace Mann was selected because he began the whole process. What the followers of Horace Mann did was based, at least in great part, on his work and his ideas.

John Dewey was considered because he became the philosopher of the Common School. His writings became the foundation for the purpose and curriculum of the public schools. For the role he played in the development of the common schools he has merited enshrinement in the hearts of public school devotees.

Charles Eliot exerted a tremendous influence on the nation in terms of his philosophy. He exerted a great influence continuing until this day. For forty years he was President of Harvard University where many teachers and administrators earned their degrees. His influence has been far reaching. He gave naturalism and materialism intellectual respectability.

William Kilpatrick was an able exponent of the real John Dewey. He was able to make practical what John Dewey had proposed in theory. Thousands of administrators and teachers were his students and have become over the years important administrators, leaders, or authors of materials used in public education, all laced with his version of Dewey.

Finally, James E. McClellan was selected because he represents in a clear way the philosopher of public education in the modern world. A brief study of his work as a modern philosopher should help us thoroughly understand that public education has an underlying explanation and that thinkers like James E. McClellan are responsible for it. McClellan expresses rather clearly what Dewey wrote rather obscurely.

It is important to mention several others that were selected by a blue ribbon committee of educators for Part II of the National Society for the Study of Education Seventeenth Yearbook.

The first of these is JOHN S. BRUBACHER (1898-)[15]. A volume which he wrote and published in 1950, *Modern Philosophies of Education*, is well known to most education students. Brubacker wrote many other books and made a significant contribution to American public education. He was a pragmatist who always considered himself a faithful follower of the philosophy of John Dewey[16]. Religiously he considered himself a Unitarian but near the end of his life he managed to elevate (?) himself to the status of a Congregationalist. Incidentally, Brubacher proved to be clearly Deweyan but also educationally ecumenical.

WILLIAM CARR (1901-1996)[17] liked to boast, in answer to a question placed by the panel in their first interview, that religion had absolutely no influence on his career. What seemed to influence Carr most was the National Educational Association. He had a theme which he constantly repeated, namely, that education was important to democracy and world citizenship.

JAMES BRYAN CONANT (1893-1978)[18] also served as President of Harvard for twenty years and spent most of his life investigating American public high schools. He was the proponent of the comprehensive high school which would provide programs and curricula for every kind of student. He opposed having students in private or parochial high schools, but, he claims, not for any church-state reason. His principal reason was that democratic education required that everyone be educated together. He was responsible for a noteworthy study of secondary education which he gave his favorite title — "Education for All American Youth."

GEORGE S. COUNTS (1889-1974)[19] was reared as a strict disciple of the Methodist Church but tells us that while he loved the hymns he did not always obey the rules. Actually he identifies himself as a Shintoist — a worshipper of nature. And indeed he was that. While he was a pragmatist in the Deweyan tradition, Counts' real faith was in education.

ARTHUR I. GATES (1890-1972)[20]. Gates pointed out in his autobiography that his family migrated to New England from England and Scotland and moved westward toward Pennsylvania and then Illinois. He mentions that they were predominantly Protestant although it is evident from his own writings that religion had little influence on his life. He admits however, he was influenced in a marked way by the works of Thorndike (thoroughly Deweyan), especially the latter's learning theories. His particular interest was evaluation methodology. Gates contributed significantly to educational testing. It is interesting to note that he worked with another member of these chosen eleven educators, Ruth Strang. Together they constructed a test on health education while they were at Columbia University. Gates was strong in his attachment to American education and to the traditions of John Dewey.

SIDNEY LEAVITT PRESSEY (1888-1979).[21] Pressey might be categorized in the same general group to which Gates belonged. He too was a beneficiary and follower of Thorndike's psychology and learning theory and became interested through this connection in doing research and evaluation in education. The child of a Congregational minister who served in the midwest, Pressey was born in Brooklyn, New York, where his father held his first appointment. Pressey summarizes these experiences by saying that many of his tasks as a minister's son were irksome but they were all educative. Pressey came to question beliefs his father preached although he admired the selfless work and devotion of his parents. Pressey worked hard in the field of testing and evaluation, an interest which was rooted in his interest in psychology. At first, he was concerned in what he called "the below normal" children. Later he began to study the advanced student, the one who was being accelerated. This interest came to him, it appears, because he was himself an advanced but non-accelerated child. At the time of his latest work he was studying the aging and had managed to produce quite a number of articles on the older generation, which he had recently joined.

The panel selected GEORGE N. SCHUSTER (1894-1977)[22]. President of Hunter College in New York from 1939 to 1960, George Schuster is the only one on the list who had a parochial school education and a Catholic higher education. He attended Notre Dame University. In 1961 when he terminated his position at Hunter he went back to Notre Dame and remained there until his retirement. He was thoroughly Catholic, making no secret about his educational or religious convictions. Schuster was, by the way, an interesting person who could captivate an audience with tales of his many experiences, especially those which took place overseas. He served in Germany as Deputy to John J. McCloy, then the United States High Commissioner to Germany. He was a personal friend of John Dewey but rejects his philosophy. His biographer states that: "Dewey's philosophy of pragmatic relativism has always been alien to Schuster's religious absolutism," and notes that Schuster maintained that in Dewey's world "relativism had become the only absolute and so made the past obsolete."

GEORGE D. STODDARD (1897-1981)[23] served as the President of the University of Illinois during the Second World War, and in the postwar period he held several important government educational positions. Stoddard's greatest claim to fame, he writes, is the authorship of "The Meaning of Intelligence" (1943). Although he managed to become a Unitarian, he states clearly that he had no regard whatever for religion. In fact, he speaks of religion as "organized superstition." One particularly biting remark comes from his autobiography: "...the decline in religious faith has had the effect of turning the attention of the paranoid to deviations seen as unpatriotic, socialist, communistic, or treasonable."

RUTH STRANG (1895-1971)[24] maintains that life is without pleasure or calamity. She had what one might call a "Quaker" outlook on life, although she claims a strict Protestant ethic acquired from her father who read the Bible every morning and every evening. Ruth Strang was a good person and a pious Protestant and led an exemplary life. Her most interesting and exciting work was performed at Teachers College, Columbia University, where she accomplished much in guidance and counseling and also specialized in reading, health education and mental health. She was a pioneer female professor who acquired a strong reputation in the field of higher education.

ROBERT ULICH (1890-1977)[25] was a German by origin and training, lacking a taste for John Dewey's philosophy and other American educational writings. Ulich did some important studies in the history of religious education and makes clear his displeasure with a growing secularism in American education and even in Church circles. He was opposed to empiricism, relativism, and environmentalism. He became irritated with American educators who he claims mistook the absence of inner-direction as a lack of progress. He criticized American classrooms for disdaining such concepts as discipline, reverence and authority. Ulich was trained in the "old German school" of strict discipline. He was committed to supporting those achievements of the public schools which were aimed at attaining the ideal for the entire nation, but at the same time used his own keen intellectual judgment to examine and disprove the philosophy of instrumentalism and pragmatism which he claimed failed to support public education because it lacked a sense of direction and did not define and articulate its own hierarchy of values. One of Ulich's greatest achievements was his desertion of Nazism — modern paganism in all its ugliness.

CARLETON WASHBURNE (1912-1968)[26] had a significant religious background and a lifelong interest in both philosophy and religion. This interest, he maintains, came from his parents. His mother had a tremendous influence on him; and his scholarly knowledge of philosophy and deep concern with religion and the religion of India became potent elements in his thoughts and feelings. Washburne joined the Quakers in the thirties because of his appreciation for what they had to offer: no official creed; no authoritative government; stress on the responsibility of every individual to follow his own inner light. His attraction to eastern religions is not clearly understandable.

The Committee in charge of developing this study on leaders in American education also included two evaluations by their own Committee members. The first evaluation was undertaken by Paul Woodring, a distinguished Service Professor of the College, Western Washington State College, Bellingham, Washington. He confined his study to the nuts and bolts of educational leadership as found in the group. Those chosen as educational leaders had their advanced degree in a variety of areas. Five of eleven had teaching experience at the elementary or secondary level; six went directly to teach at the college level. None were from a "wealthy" family and none were from a "disadvantaged" family. No Afro-Americans and only one woman were among the eleven chosen. No information was available on their intellectual standing, such as I.Q.'s or other psychological data. Woodring notes that it is clear that all the educators were very intelligent and all of them were prolific writers.

Robert L. McCaul[27], an associate professor of education at the University of Chicago, wrote the most interesting evaluation. Reference has been made in the early parts of this study to "public school leaders." McCaul hesitates to speak of them as leaders. Instead, he speaks of them as "eleven eminent educators." He makes clear that they are not in the category of those who brought about great changes in public education. Such were educators of the calibre of Dewey, Thorndike, Judd, Kandell, Terman, and Cubberly. The latter were responsible for enormous changes in the public educational system. These "eminent" leaders are all from the second half of the nineteenth century and what seems to be implied in this judgment is that they began to lead public education out of the complications in which Horace Mann left the system. They moved it toward the system recognized today in our country as "public or American education."

McCaul refers to these eleven eminent educators as ones who did not set into motion forces that destroyed "old orthodoxies and ushered in new ones. They did not revolutionize old fields of study…they did not create new fields of educational study like educational psychology, or human development. Mostly they elaborated, applied, and improved, frequently with extraordinary brilliance and inventiveness, the ideas, techniques, and structures they had inherited from their predecessors."

McCaul then goes on to discuss how these eminent educators should be viewed in terms of their links to the past and relation to the future. Gates, Pressey, and Strang were, he states, beneficiaries of Thorndike's contribution to learning theory and to research and evaluation methodology; Counts was a legatee of Dewey's reconstructionism and Washburne of Dewey's progressivism.

McCaul then goes on to say that Brubacher wrote educational philosophy in a pre-Deweyan mode, as well as in the Deweyan mode. One who is familiar with the early histories of philosophy as well as Brubacher's efforts can attest to the truth of this observation. Brubacher studied the traditionally accepted philosophies of education. As a matter of fact one would search in vain to find anything like McClellan's

"First Philosophy" in Brubacher's work. Brubacher does, however, follow the John Dewey philosophy but still does not hesitate to refer to St. Thomas Aquinas. As a matter of fact Brubacher even uses St. Thomas and Dewey in the same sentence. "In fact the ultimate test of any conclusion is its success in getting itself accepted by competent students in the field. Although the natural order is very matter of fact, it nevertheless is not wanting in a certain sublimity. Plato and his Republic, St. Thomas and his De Magistro, Dewey and his Democracy and Education, were all products of nature, perennially stimulating gifts to unnumbered teachers yet to come."[28] One could discuss the adequacy of Brubacher's statement for some time but the monumental thing about it is the positive inclusion of such an array of unlikely authors and scholars in the same sentence, something which had been outlawed by Dewey and his faithful followers for years. Brubacher even speaks of the two ways of learning or knowing and maintains they are not mutually exclusive or antagonistic to each other. He was eager to bring some consensus about dealing with learning the secular curriculum. Not everyone would accept the Brubacher proposal.

Conant tried to improve existing educational structures. He certainly did not try to change them much less to eradicate them.

Carr fits into this group nicely because he was concerned with teachers and especially classroom teachers. He conducted the NEA in accordance with "what might be called a nineteenth century American Common School ideology of collegiality and consensus."

Schuster and Ulich do not fit in the group already mentioned. Schuster was an outspoken Catholic. He attended Catholic schools from the beginning, finally achieving the office of administrative assistant to the President of Notre Dame University. Having been educated at that University he began an extraordinary career in the field of education even to the point of being recognized as a leader in American education in this 70th NSSE Yearbook.

Ulich was very much upset by Dewey and the pragmatism which dominated American education and life, believing it would be a good thing if some German idealism could impact American education.

McCaul singles out for special notice George Stoddard, viewing him, unlike the other ten eminent educators, as a greater force in American education. Stoddard, he maintains, raised important questions about American education; he moved it from a study of "nature" to an emphasis on "nurture." His work with testing and particularly his evaluations and measures of intelligence have moved American education a long way, for it became dominant during the fifties and, as McCaul states, it is likely to remain a long time.

Two different characteristics of this study should be noted. The one includes ten of the eminent educators listed above. What these did according to McCaul was to strengthen, to polish, and to elevate existing ideas and concepts in American education. They did not change the old order. They did not create any new movements or great ideas, but they did improve them.

Stoddard, on the other hand, according to McCaul, did shake the educational world by his work, especially by his book on *The Meaning of Intelligence.*[29] McCaul also points out that Stoddard made important studies of nature and nurture and for these reasons he classifies him at a higher level than the other ten eminent educators.

These brief summaries of the outstanding American educators, made an effort to discover their association, if any, with religion. Primarily such an effort followed a question submitted to each educator: "The bearing of your experience with religion on your career." That question about religion may seem strange and even out of place. However, a little thoughtful review may help us understand more clearly.

This 1970 Yearbook was published in the same decade as the Schempp Case (1963) which repudiated the role of religion in public education almost totally. Strangely enough, American education's most basic concept in the development of the Common School (the Public School) was clearly that religion belonged in education according to American social tradition[3.0]

In Horace Mann's final report covering 1848, he wrote a lengthy defense of his position on religion in public education:

Morality, he conceded, is unattainable without religion, and no community will ever be religious without religious education. Devoid of religious principles, the race can sink to great depths; enlightened by them, it can rise higher and higher. Yet, in this area, as in others, it must be education. "...If man be not a religious being," he continued "he is among the most deformed and monstrous of all possible existences."

"... I avail myself of this, the last opportunity which I may ever have, to say, in regard to all affirmations or intimations, that I have ever attempted to exclude religious instruction from school, or to exclude the Bible from school, or to impair the force of that volume, arising out of itself, are now, and always have been, without substance or semblance of truth."[31]

Since this study maintains that the real conflict in American education is precisely about the role of religion, the educators' religious affiliations or non-affiliations, as well as the degree of religious influence in his or her work, were considered and evaluated in so far as possible.

Three recognized religious educators were on the panel who made the selections: William W. Brickman, a prominent Orthodox Jewish educator; Neil McClusky, S.J., a Jesuit education scholar and widely known in the field of education; and P. C. Reinert, S.J., an outstanding Jesuit educator and then President of St. Louis University.

These three and perhaps others would almost automatically suggest the "religion" question. Perhaps others joined them. Others would know about the early history of this issue and the continuing controversy between religion and education in America. With the Supreme Court action in Schempp (1963) and the extraordinary negative reaction to that decision, the question was a natural.

The eleven candidates had a chronological age range from 70 to 82 which indicates that their most active and productive period was during the most intense periods of the religion-education conflict. The invitational letter indicated — "candidates must be born before 1901, so they will be 70 or over in 1971, when the Yearbook will be published."[32]

For these and many other reasons the question of religion was a natural. There was (1) the famous guidelines established by Horace Mann, determining that "Religion belonged"; that (2) Catholicism was definitely out; that (3) Sectarianism needs to be excluded; (4) the endless religious conflicts, climaxing in the Supreme Court decisions in the matter of Everson (1947), McCollum (1948), and the Supreme Court decision "closing" the subject with Schempp (1963).

Our findings in this regard follow closely McCaul's division of eminent educators. Schuster, Ulich, and Stoddard do indeed break the mold. Schuster is an absolutely unusual selection for this study. He is a very dedicated Catholic gentleman who had no time for John Dewey, a fact he readily admits. Ulich, although he does not admit any particular religious affiliation, does maintain his disapproval of the pragmatism that he discovered in American life and education. Stoddard on the other hand turns out to be the exemplar, the shining example among the eleven educators. The work he did is considered by McCaul as almost pioneer work. He opened new fields of study; he led American education in new directions and to higher levels.

As a youth Stoddard lived a formally Methodist life. He went to church, avoided games on Sunday, and as he indicates, the colored comics, but when he became twelve years old (sic) began to answer in his own way the age-old question of man's relation to the universe and his fellowman: "thus it was an easy step to Unitarianism."[33] In his autobiography, after stating that his social ideas are very liberal, Stoddard writes the following most interesting insights into his social ideas:

> All we children had to do was to apply a touch of reason and the scientific approach to witness a quick deflation of dogma. It became clear that to behave properly through fear of semi-eternal or eternal punishment, and for no other reason, was in itself a shameful human condition…My young mind was asked to believe that the more vague and subjective the "sin" the more certain and horrible the retribution. Children who could read learned that for centuries organized religion had found easy ways, through money or repentance, of absolving a person of guilt and its dreadful consequence. Through an intense interest all through college in the mechanism of heredity, I applied the same thought processes to the question of life-after-death, a personal God, the revealed Truth, and all that. As with the soul itself, no entity, condition, structure, or necessity was revealed. The whole structure was so obviously humanoid as to make the inquiry itself irrational and fruitless. Beyond adolescence and throughout adulthood I retained a sense of wonder toward unan-

swerable questions about the universe, the galaxies, the physical forces at work, and the emergence of life itself. Long before I ran into the term teleology I rejected its implications....agnosticism, ethical culture, or Unitarianism are not tickets to preferment in the ranks of academic administrators, although tolerance is on the upswing. The commonest religion of all, namely "no religious preference," is in fashion and sustains an aura of open-mindedness.[34]

Reflecting on some activity in his new religious environment Stoddard regarded it as a "valuable counterpoise to the pressures of organized superstition." From Stoddard's writings one can understand why he was named a leader in American education.

REFLECTIONS

This study of leaders in American education is given for several reasons. First it should indicate to all of us that public education is not wanting for leaders. American education has been blessed with great authors, great statesmen, great organizers. Public education could not exist without them. On the other hand, one must be struck by the lack of import which religion held in their eyes. The majority dismissed religion as unimportant.

What is typical in the lives of these eminent educators is that religion does not have an important role to play, neither in education nor in life. Horace Mann believed that religion was important to education and it "belonged" in education. That belief has long since — in great measure — disappeared. Those public educational leaders who did accept religion as a part of their life kept it in its place. They joined, principally it seemed, the Unitarian Church, which theologically and religiously, can be classified with the religion of Emily Post. Even if they had this abbreviated form of religion, or perhaps something a step higher, what they reflected in their own life and certainly in their educational writings was this: religion is not an important part of life, it has nothing to do with public life or behavior; it is something that you can take or leave; it is not important to the individual nor to society. The supernatural has come to mean the amazing things performed by David Copperfield and other illusionists. The dictionary defines "illusion" as the state or fact of being intellectually deceived or misled. The "supernatural" level, revelation, the soul, grace, and the remainder of religion" is simply "organized superstition."

Stoddard, it will be noted, was singled out as more than a mere educational leader because he "set in motion forces destroying old orthodoxies and ushering in new ones" and because he "revolutionized old fields of study."

Stoddard was the ideal in that group of "eminent educators" because he called a spade a spade and wore his Dewey button on his sleeve. After his personal study of man's relation to the universe and to his fellowman, Stoddard found it "an easy step to Unitarianism." He indicates that he has had some involvement in religion and notes that this "degree of commitment, if not more,…I still regard as a valuable counterpoise to the pressures of organized superstitions." The message is clear.

It is suggested that the "real" educational leader thinks religion is nonsense and gets involved in it (Stoddard's degree of commitment) because it is "a valuable counterpoise to the pressures of organized superstitions." That, it would seem, applies the basic philosophy of pragmatism and instrumentalism to religion.

From the Catholic point of view religion and the supernatural are not considered a meaningless counterpoise; they are essential aspects of life. Religion must be a part of the whole man — that reality we must understand if we are to attain any meaningful understanding of life. From the Catholic view it is not an unfortunate, meaningless non-entity in life. It is of the essence of life. The religious aspect of one's life is not to be kept hidden under a basket. It is to be developed just as the physical, the intellectual, and the social, and it is to be a proud, public, meaningful aspect of what life is all about.

It is suggested that the absence of religion in one's life, or its diminution to almost nothing, is a prominent characteristic of many leaders in public education. Thus the explanation of life and reality through scientific methods and the elimination of bothersome moral laws are more readily accomplished. It does explain what Syndey Hook meant when he labeled every philosophy in the field "garrulous absurdities" except his own.

Today, because of the Schempp Case, religion in American education does not exist. American education is truly secular and godless, as the naturalistic educational leaders in this country have proposed from its beginning. While they did noble work in many ways and while they were factors in the establishment of the great American educational system, there is no denying that their work ignored and eventually eliminated the essential role of religion in our life. This problem must concern us seriously. The lack of religion in the life of our people has brought a grave crisis into our lives, and we must wonder whether or not American life will be able to survive as it should. First, can life be completely and properly understood without religion? and second, can a meaningful education program be constructed without religion?

CONCLUSIONS

The crisis began as a conflict between religious groups and the backers of Horace Mann's Common School Movement. The only group to lose out on the first round of this tremendous conflict were Catholics. They were generally unacceptable to the population and particularly to Horace Mann. When it came to planning a common school, everyone could be considered for a role except the Catholic Church and its schools. A common form of Protestantism is what Horace Mann desired and so he created it. The Bible and the principle of "private judgment," the most fundamental criteria of Protestantism, would be the sole guide for Mann's religion in the common schools.[35]

Other religious groups would lose the next round in the contest. Horace Mann indicated that religion was important in the education of children but that sectarianism was to be rejected absolutely. As the various sects walked away angry, Horace Mann set down and developed his own version — a nonsectarian version of the Protestant religion.

From the beginning of education in this country, Catholics have had a serious problem defending their schools. In the opening Chapter of this brief study, the history of the prejudice and hatred of Catholics and their schools was traced up to a Supreme Court decision — the Pierce Case in 1925. What the Catholics were trying to solve first was: could their schools exist legally with their particular brand of religion? In that famous case in 1925, the question was answered clearly and affirmatively by the Supreme Court.

Horace Mann's new religion and subsequent Protestant reinforcements of it became a bone of contention throughout the history of public education until 1963. On June 17 of that year the Supreme Court answered Horace Mann's question finally and decisively. There would be no room in the public schools even for Mann's modified version of Protestanism. Horace Mann, who first eliminated from education Catholicism and then all Protestant sectarianism except his own version, lost even those small vestiges of religion. The Schempp Case confirmed that the schools which he had been so instrumental in creating would now be without any religion.

The reaction to this Supreme Court decision was incredible. The ruling "…provoked a massive public outcry and has met with steady resistance since (its) announcement. Outright noncompliance with the decisions at the local level has been considerable. In addition, a number of states have simply enacted laws authorizing voluntary spoken prayer, in defiance of the decisions. Proponents of school prayer have long argued for a constitutional amendment specifically authorizing voluntary organized prayer in public schools."[36]

So the struggle of the Catholics to survive ended with the Pierce Case (1925). The struggle of the Protestant public schools to survive, and the struggle initiated by John Dewey and his followers, ended unhappily in 1963 for the Protestant religion followers of Mann, but happily and on target for John Dewey and his followers. The Schempp Case ended with the total legal ban on all religious devotions, practices, simple prayers, or readings in the public schools of the nation.

Religion has been at the eye of the public education whirlwind which began with Horace Mann. The Catholics moved ahead one small step in 1925. The Protestants have moved back one giant step in 1963.

At one time it could have been said that the majority in the United States believed, as did Mann, that religion "belonged in the education of youth." Whether that can be said now is unlikely. Secularism or some other form of materialism has become the official and favored "religion" in our country. Those who are in favor of this "new religion" back it up with loud support and with lives that reflect exactly what their new beliefs maintain.

The battle in education has been about religion, it is still about religion, and it will probably continue to be about religion. In light of this would it not be better for our leaders, both educational and civil, to find a solution to the real problem that exists, not only in our minds and hearts, but in reality? Has there been some miscalculation?

NOTES

1) *Catholic Encyclopedia*, Vol. 5, 274; cf. Jeffrey O'Connell, *Naturalism in American Education* (New York: Benzinger Bros., 1938), 86 ff.

2) O'Connell, chapter 5.

3) ibid., 145, 149, 152.

4) ibid., 152.

5) James E. McClellan, "First Philosophy in Education" (80th Yearbook, NSSE), 1981, chapter XI, 263.

6) ibid., 263.

7) ibid., 265.

8) ibid., 268.

9) ibid., 268.

10) ibid., 275.

11) ibid., 285.

12) ibid., 286 ff.

13) 71st Yearbook NSSE, Part 1, 1972, 192.

14) 70th Yearbook NSSE, Part 2, 1971.

15) ibid., 17.

16) ibid., 48.

17) ibid., 65.

18) ibid., 113.

19) ibid., 151.

20) ibid., 189.

21) ibid., 231.

22) ibid., 277.

23) ibid., 321.

24) ibid., 365.

25) ibid., 413.

26) ibid., 417.

27) ibid., 500-504 ff.

28) Brubacher, John S., *Modern Philosophies of Education*
(New York: McGraw-Hill, 1950), 332.

29) 70th Yearbook NSSE, Part 2, 1971, 343 and 349-350. Stoddard does not hesitate to boast that his book *The Meaning of Intelligence*, Macmillan, New York, 1943
was the high point of his life. McCaul apparently agrees with that evaluation. Few
others do. On p. 4 of that book he gives this definition: "Intelligence is the ability
to undertake activities that are characterized by (1) difficulty, (2) complexity, (3)
abstractness, (4) economy, (5) adaptiveness to a goal, (6) social value, and (7) the
emergence of originals, and to maintain such activities under conditions that
demand a concentration of energy and a resistance to emotional forces. Cf.
Timothy Gannon, *Psychology: The Unity of Human Behavior,* Ginn and Company,
Boston, 1954, 343 ff.

30) Dunn, William K., *What Happened to Religious Education,* (Baltimore: John
Hopkins Press, 1958) 116.

31) ibid., 143-147 passim.

32) 71st Yearbook NSSE, Part 2, 4.

33) Unitarianism required no dogma, no creed; differing opinions are encouraged
as the most likely source of new and better understanding. Worship is non-liturgi-
cal. God is not conceived as a supernatural being, but as a force for good, visible in
the power and beauty of nature; there is no Trinity and Jesus is not the unique Son
of God or Redeemer. There is no Supernatural, Revelation, Grace, Redemption, etc.

34) 70th Yearbook NSSE, Part 2, 1971, 324, 333, 334.

35) Dunn, 259.

36) "Origins and Historical Understanding of the Free Exercise of Religion," 103;
Harvard Law Review (May 1990), 1661.

CHAPTER 8

Supreme Court Decisions — Part A

Pierce v. Society of Sisters answered some important questions for the entire American community. From that famous decision it was now possible to maintain: 1) that the Supreme Court recognized that parents are the primary educators of their children; 2) that parents had the first choice of the kind of school they wanted for their children. They could not be compelled to send their children to public school despite the Compulsory Education Laws.[1] They did, however, have the obligation of providing the conditions of education called for by laws regulating properly qualified schools of their own choice.

The settlement of these matters was of supreme importance, not only for parents, but also for other citizens as well as civil authorities. It placed Catholic and other religious educational programs beyond the dark shadow of suspicion which had been their earlier fate. In 1792, when the State of New Hampshire forbade tax funds to any denominational school and continuing until the Oregon State Case in 1925, there was always some doubt about the integrity of non-public schools in this country. During that long period, religious schools, especially Catholic, were looked upon as divisive intruders and less than American. Little effort was made to understand why people would make such sacrifices and go to such great extremes to provide a religiously oriented education for their children.

These suspicions became even greater after the Common School was established. Now education was available for all people. The Common School founders believed this to be truly American education. Yet Catholics and certain other religious groups continued to make tremendous sacrifices in order to provide their own religiously oriented education for their children. From its origin in the time of Horace Mann until the Schempp Case, 1963, the public school also offered religion (Mann's version) in its curriculum. Religious schools and religious education therefore were not an unusual offering on the American education scene.

Study of the history of that period makes clear precisely why such sacrifices were made. The public schools, especially under the influence of Horace Mann, John Dewey, and many of his prize students, were clearly anti-Catholic, but not always anti-religious. This fact was reflected in the textbooks which were put into the hands of children and in the many insults hurled over the years at "Papists." Other religions seemed to escape the sharp criticism given Catholics. The truth was that the engineers of the public school were opposed to all sectarianism but they had a special distaste for Catholics. Indeed public school founders did not accept religion except in some very modified, watered-down way.

A more cutting charge was the allegation that Catholics were incapable of being good American citizens. Despite all the evidence to the contrary, leading public school officials as well as government officials continued to maintain that there was no room for "Papists" in the United States. The Pierce v. Society of Sisters Case came before the Supreme Court precisely because the Masonic Order and the Ku Klux Klan were anxious to make the Catholics and their schools disappear. This is one of the main reasons why Catholics rejoiced in the 1925 Supreme Court decision. If it settled anything at all, and it did, it determined legally the role of parents in education in the United States. The existence of Catholic schools in this country, as long as they fulfilled the legal requirements of the State, was forever justified.[2]

But other questions had to be answered before this debate could be considered settled. Would the State support financially the parents who would not send their children to Protestant religious public schools but preferred to educate them in another sort of approved school? Would the State help provide funds to support forms of non-public education chosen by parents whose right to do so had been so forcefully and clearly declared constitutional by the Supreme Court? Or would this right deteriorate into a mere unusable privilege even though such schools met all the requirements of the Civil authorities? Would the State help support the right of parents to educate their children religiously, according to their own conscience? Or would the State give consent for the schools and give nothing for their support? The Pierce v. Society of Sisters decision did not indicate that Catholics were now accepted by their fellow citizens or that their schools would be funded by the government.

The reputation of Catholics was clearly demonstrated in the story of Alfred E. Smith, who in 1928 became the Democratic nominee for President.[3] His is a story of political obscurity to prominence. When he was thirteen years old his father died and from that time he supported his mother and sister. Because of his family situation he was unable to receive a normal education and frequently described himself, jokingly, as a graduate of the Fulton Fish Market.

Despite all his personal difficulties, Smith rose to be Governor of New York State and in 1928 he became the Democratic nominee for the presidency.

The big issue — the only issue — was his Catholicism. Many openly believed that his religion disqualified him for the presidency. In May 1927 Al Smith issued the following statement: "I believe in absolute freedom of conscience for all men and in equality of all churches and sects, all beliefs before the law as a matter of right and not as a matter of favor." But there was deep and vicious anti-Catholic bias in the land, which proved to be too much for the candidate. He was overwhelmingly defeated in the election.

The Al Smith period made it clear that the Church would never win a popularity contest in the United States. The same bigotry that Catholics experienced throughout the 19th century and into the 20th century was still rampant.

Naturally the church and the Catholic school issue had to be solved in some other way. The Pierce v. Society of Sisters Case had taught a great lesson. Perhaps this would involve the judiciary as the division of the Federal Government to which Catholics should appeal. It certainly would be free of the whims, ambitions and fancies of politicians where countless pressure and prejudices were exerted daily in an effort to move officials one way or the other. Most of all it would be the highest level of the Judiciary — the Supreme Court — the level noted for its scholarship, its fairness, and its unblemished character. Certainly this Court would not be touched by the evils of bigotry. This distinguished body of scholars was considered untouchable, it was thought, and they would be the final arbiters of any legal puzzles facing the nation. Here was the obvious jury to make such important decisions.

One can imagine what thoughts and dreams ran through the minds of Catholics during that period from 1925 to 1944. Maybe this horrible nightmare of humiliating bigotry over Catholics and their schools, if placed in the hands of the Supreme Court as the final arbiter, could be settled fairly once and for all.

THE COCHRAN CASE[4]
In 1929 the State of Louisiana passed a law which gave free textbooks to those who attended not only public schools but any qualified school in the State. The Supreme Court of the State of Louisiana upheld this law. Eventually it was appealed to the United States Supreme Court. The Court ruled that the law granting free textbooks to all children regardless of their creed, or their school, was constitutional.

In all there were six states authorizing the distribution of non-sectarian textbooks: Alabama, Indiana, Kansas, Louisiana, Mississippi, and West Virginia. In subsequent years some states reneged on the practice; but other states passed laws providing free textbooks for all children. The State of Mississippi noted in its decision these memorable words: "The State is under the order to ignore the child's creed, but not its need."

In 1946 the Federal Government declared "The National School Lunch Act" which had the specific purpose of serving all children "...as a measure of national security to safeguard the health and well being of the nation's children and to encourage domestic consumption of nutritious agricultural commodities and other foods, by assisting the State, through grants-in-aid and other means, in providing an adequate supply of food and other facilities for the establishment, maintenance, operation and expansion of school lunch programs." In the Act, school was defined clearly: "School" means any public or non-profit private school, high school, grade or under (Section 4).[5]

This was of course wonderful news for the schools, especially non-public schools. Indeed the Supreme Court, both in its actions and its deliberations from the Pierce Case and throughout the thirties, insured the kind and just treatment of our schools by the federal government in the National School Lunch Act and the Cochran Case. These were special moments in American Catholic life.

In the meantime, another World War had come and gone. Hitler rose to power in Germany in 1933. From that date numerous warlike acts involving Italy, Japan, and Germany served as a prelude to another horrendous conflict, World War II. Throughout this period President Roosevelt made one plea after another to convince the Axis Powers to maintain peace, but to no avail. On December 7, 1941 Japan attacked our fleet at Pearl Harbor. It was a staggering military loss for our nation. The enemy destroyed or disabled nineteen ships; 120 planes were destroyed on the ground, and more than 2400 men and officers lost their lives.

The next day the President came before Congress and asked for a Declaration of War. That terrible disaster known as World War II followed. In all 256,330 were killed in battle; entire towns and nations were wiped out; millions of civilians, men, women, and children, were killed during that period. It was the worst conflict the world had thus far witnessed, exceeding in horror even World War I. Terrible events took place during this encounter, such as the Holocaust, in which Hitler and his followers destroyed some six million Jews, among others.

American soldiers fought for their freedom and that of the whole world. They fought in many locations in Europe and the Pacific. Tales of their bravery and honor are still related to this day. White, Negro, Catholic, Protestant, and Jew — public school graduates along with religious school graduates — stood side by side to secure world freedom and justice. These men bought, at times with their own lives, our precious freedoms. The Germans surrendered in May 1945 and the Japanese gave up September 2, 1945.

What stupendous victories. Within days of the surrender many of the boys made their way home. They came home arm in arm to a fairly settled situation. The country was waiting for them and gave them a stupendous welcome. Various plans to help them resettle were awaiting. Among the best known was the G.I. Bill of Rights (1944). Among other benefits the returning veterans could receive free tuition and books to a college of their choice or, if they wished, another form of advanced education. An estimated 7.8 million veterans took advantage of this program, costing the country about 14.5 billion dollars.

It was in this happy context that the decision was made to take the schools issue to the Supreme Court, first the auxiliary aid and then the direct aid. Key to the outcome of this appeal would be the Supreme Court's understanding and interpretation of these few words:

"Congress shall make no law respecting an establishment of Religion or prohibit the free exercise thereof."[6]

What happened during the next few months is almost incomprehensible. In undertaking the Everson Bus Case in February 1947 and the McCollum Case in

October 1947, this exalted Court of the United States turned back the calendar over a hundred years to the time of the Know-Nothings. What they did to those two lines from the Bill of Rights is astounding: they changed words; they misinterpreted them; they gave them new meanings; they distorted them beyond recognition; they wrote new laws; they converted them into a new First Amendment to make it impossible for the religious schools' parents to receive any financial help from their country.

The Catholics were again reduced to second-rate citizens by the Supreme Court. The Justices showed themselves as uneducated men who knew little of their own history, culture, or Constitution, but remembered only and exploited the prejudices of their own countrymen. This Court did so much damage that it will take years to recover from their insidious, biased, unscholarly, insulting, and shameful interpretation of these few lines of the First Amendment. Like the Know-Nothings, they said, in effect, "Go back where you came from. This is not your home."

THE BILL OF RIGHTS

The Constitution was approved in 1789 and ratified two years later in 1791. In that same year the Bill of Rights was also enacted. Those ten Amendments to the Constitution were intended as safeguards to the States who had delegated authority to the Federal Government. What the States wanted to retain they did not delegate to the Federal Government. Thus, nothing is mentioned about education in the Federal Constitution. This would be the domain of the States alone. It was clear, however, that the Federal Government would have no authority to make any sort of national church or religion; all religions would be treated equally, not ignored. At that time there were nine established churches among the Colonies: six were Anglican or Episcopal and three were Congregational; none was Catholic. The Constitution states only one thing about religion and the Federal Government: that it shall make no religious test as a qualification for office.[7]

Many immigrants came to this country to escape an established church. Their experience with such governmental arrangements had always been negative and they wanted no more of it. When the Catholics (both German and Irish) were deserted by the French in 1758 and the English soldiers took over at the former Fort Duquesne (now Pittsburgh), the English Church and law also took over. Prior to 1758 the settlers possessed a fortress with a chapel and Catholic chaplains which was open to all people. When England took over, it excluded the Catholic chapel and chaplains. In fact, Catholics were not allowed to vote, nor were they allowed to own property. Catholics were not allowed to serve in the Militia, but they were fined for failing to do so. In 1776, the people had enough government interference in the management of their colonies. They had come to the colonies to escape many problems, especially the one identified as "an establishment of religion."

The Bill of Rights recognized this clearly in the First Amendment. "Congress shall make no law respecting an establishment of religion." Hence, there will be no federal national church, no federal official church, no federal official religion. All persons were free to practice the religion which they chose.[8]

An official religion, one which would be preferred over all others, was forbidden by the States when they delegated authority to the Federal Government. The old, strict literal sense of union between government and a single religion was prevented by the First Amendment forever.

O'Neill has done a magnificent analysis of this entire problem. O'Neill chaired the Department of Speech at Brooklyn College. Incidentally, for twelve years he was a member and for four years the Chairman of the Committee on Academic Freedom of the American Civil Liberties Union. His book is entitled *Religion and Education under the Constitution*, an excellent source for information on this subject. Unfortunately it is too late to ask the Supreme Court Justices to read it. It gives a thorough summary and interpretation of what the First Amendment is all about. Here is a quotation from the beginning of his book:

> The First Amendment, particularly so far as its first phrase is concerned — "Congress shall make no law respecting an establishment of religion" — does not express any attitude whatever toward religion. It expresses no principle whatever of Catholicism, Protestantism, Judaism, Shintoism, or Atheism. It was meant to express and does express the wishes of the people who wrote it, adopted it, and ratified it, in regard to a specific problem in the delegation of powers by the people of the country to the federal government. The federal government is a government of delegated powers. It has no power except that which the people have given it through legally adopted constitutional provisions.
>
> The phrase "Congress shall make no law respecting an establishment of religion" is a simple, specific prohibition of action by Congress in regard to a specific subject. It is a "keep out" sign. It seeks to make explicit what Hamilton in the "Federalist," and Madison in his letter to Thomas Jefferson of October 17, 1788, and Jefferson in his reply to Madison's letter of March 5, 1789, all substantially agreed was implicit in the constitutional relationship between the individual states and the federal government when the original Constitution was ratified. This phrase was not put into the Constitution to make any new arrangement. It was simply to make what was the essential situation at the time so clearly and specifically stated that no one in the future could question what the situation was; namely, that the question of "an establishment of religion" for the whole United States by the Congress of the United States was a subject which Congress should not touch. It neither approved nor disapproved of the established religions then existing in the individual states. It made explicit the fact that Congress was powerless to act in favor of an establishment of religion for the nation. At the time there was no national establishment

of religion. Obviously, therefore, there could never be one if Congress could never legislate on the subject. The phraseology finally adopted after long discussion accomplished the exact purpose of preventing a national church from taking the place of the dying state churches, and at the same time made possible the support of the Bill of Rights by those who still believed in state-established churches.

Various religious writers, both Catholic and Protestant, have within the last decade sought to find in the First Amendment some expression of religious, theological, or ecclesiastical doctrine. I submit that these are all futile searches. There is no such doctrine in the First Amendment. It is a purely political provision dealing with the allocation of legislative authority in regard to a specific topic. It is impossible to find any other meaning ascribed to it in the writings or official record of Jefferson or Madison. The Justices of the Supreme Court in their "interpretation" of the First Amendment in the two cases Everson and McCollum have not accurately quoted a single such passage or cited a single such fact. Neither have the two press releases, nor the manifestos issued to date (June, 1948) by "Protestants and Other Americans United." There is no such passage or fact to be found in the many letters to the press, speeches to various organizations, etc., issued in recent years by others who have been trying to get the First Amendment out of their way.[9]

Misunderstanding about the relationship of the Fourteenth Amendment to the First Amendment has recently emerged in the writings of those opposed to non-public school aid. For a complete analysis of this, consult O'Neill. In Chapter 10 of his book he makes a careful study of the relationship of the Fourteenth to the First Amendment and demonstrates that it does not affect the First Amendment. The Fourteenth Amendment was passed in 1868 and makes no practical difference in understanding of the Bill of Rights in the above case.

THE EVERSON CASE[10]

Attempts to extend aid to non-public schools were continually made by the parents of the children who attended them. Practically speaking, they recognized that such help would be needed if these schools were to survive. Their first effort was to seek auxiliary aid.

In 1941 the New Jersey State Legislature enacted a law which would entitle non-public school students, along with all other students, to receive free bus transportation. The State Courts rejected the first challenge made by a taxpayer named Everson. The New Jersey Supreme Court ruled that the Bus Statute was constitutional. Everson then appealed to the United States Supreme Court.

There are two aspects to this Case which must be noted. First, the Supreme Court responded with a favorable decision to the New Jersey law. Justice Hugo Black, representing the majority of the Court, indicated that this transportation aid did not violate the First Amendment of the Constitution. That response came in 1947. Second, although the response was favorable for the children attending non-public schools, Justice Black used the occasion to make the First Amendment read the way he thought it should. He established a meaning and interpretation of the First Amendment to the Constitution which was neither expected nor justified. He employed the words of Jefferson that the First Amendment was intended "to erect a wall of separation between Church and State." So while concluding that the New Jersey Law did not scale "the wall" in the Bus Case, Justice Black, at the same time, did grave harm by inserting his own absolute separation theory between religion and government through his metaphorical and fallacious interpretation of the First Amendment.

By placing an interpretation on that Law that can be categorized as favoring *absolute and complete separation*, Black accomplished several things. First, he broke off the brief history of a friendly, cooperative, practical interpretation of that First Amendment to describe the relationship between religion and government. Second, he closed off an important avenue of discussion and dialogue which one day could have helped non-public school parents and their children to share in the benefits of their tax support of education.

Scholars generally agreed that Justice Black was not very well acquainted with the writings of Jefferson. The only other possible conclusion is that Black deliberately made this extraordinary error in interpreting the Everson Case which caused millions of parents and children to suffer from a disastrous misinterpretation of the First Amendment. It put the religious community right where the majority of bigots wanted it to be.

The fact is, of course, that Jefferson did use the expression "a wall of separation between Church and State."[11] He used the expression in a courteous reply which he made as President of the United States to a letter written by a Committee representing the Danbury, Connecticut, Baptist Association. Jefferson wrote it on January 1, 1802. On that occasion, he was addressing in a friendly way a problem the Baptist Association was facing in their own home State. Jefferson wanted to assure them that even though they had been insulted and ignored by the Civil Government of Connecticut, the matter would be straightened out in days to come. He assured them that there was a wall of separation between all religions and the national government and that no preferential treatment could be given to or imposed on any particular form of religion. Jefferson wrote this note thirteen years after he worked on the First Amendment of the Constitution. Careful historians see absolutely no connection between the First Amendment and this metaphor which has now become a menace in all interpretations of relationships between government and religion. Justice Black lifted this metaphor out of its proper context. He found it in one of the many brief courteous responses which President Jefferson had written, and elevated it to the dignity of the First Amendment of the Bill of Rights.

The most thorough analysis of this problem will be found, as mentioned, in O'Neill's book. O'Neill often makes a line-by-line analysis of the egregious errors committed by Justice Black. Anyone who is interested in the true meaning of our Constitution should know about the mistakes which were made.[12]

Rutledge, an associate of Black's, quotes the Statute for Establishing Religious Freedom for the State of Virginia and concludes that Jefferson and Madison could never approve the New Jersey Law. The lack of logic is so shameful that it is embarrassing. To think that a Supreme Court Justice would not know that what Jefferson and Madison did about the State of Virginia Constitution would be clearly distinct from what they did as authors of the Federal Constitution and its Ten Amendments! To think that Rutledge would not realize that Jefferson and Madison understood that the laws of New Jersey cannot be judged by the Constitution of Virginia. This confusion comes from Justice Rutledge — an alleged legal expert, a supposed scholar in law, and a Justice of the highest Court in the land.

But as O'Neill points out, Rutledge makes more errors.

"The passages which seem to indicate what Justice Rutledge thinks 'an establishment of religion' means in the First Amendment are two, one in his text and one in footnote 34 (in the Supreme Court Text). In the first he says that a threat to maintaining that complete and permanent separation of religion and civil power which the First Amendment commands is through the use of the taxing power to support religion, religious establishments, or establishments having a religious foundation, whatever their form or special religious function. Here Justice Rutledge may mean either of two things: (1) that 'establishment' means 'taxing power to support religion or religious establishments,' or (2) that 'an establishment of religion' means 'religion, religious establishments, or establishments having a religious foundation, whatever their form or special religious function' — in other words any religious organization or institution or establishment (as a commercial establishment, an educational establishment, a financial establishment)."[13]

The solution of this case has been simple. First, you define the Amendment to mean what you want it to mean. Then you solve your problem on the basis of your own misunderstanding. Rutledge does this when he considers the financial aspects of the problem. Establishment, he writes, is public support of religion. No place in the First Amendment, in those sixteen little words, is there any mention of tax, money, finance, or anything resembling those words.

As O'Neill states so clearly: "The first clause of the First Amendment cannot legitimately have the slightest bearing on any law that treats all religions alike in the matter of taxation or anything else. Equality of all religions and freedom in the exercise of all religions nationally were the two objectives of the First Amendment, and the only objectives in the purpose of its creators."[14]

THE McCOLLUM CASE

One year after the Everson Bus Case, a new problem was brought before the Supreme Court. This has become known as the McCollum Case. In summary, priests, ministers and rabbis of Champaign, Illinois, began a released time program in 1940.[15] The program gave children from grades four to eight religious instruction of their choice. For thirty minutes each week, representatives of each religion came into the public school, held class with those children who chose to be in their rooms and had the permission of their parents to do so. The mother of one poor child, though a professed atheist, wanted her child to have nothing to do with this program. He was allowed to do something else during that half hour, but his mother alleged that he was ridiculed because he remained alone and away from released time class.

Because the local Circuit Court and the Illinois Supreme Court dismissed her petition, she appealed to the United States Supreme Court. The decision was written by Justice Hugo Black of Everson fame. Naturally, he would decide this case on the basis of his own unique interpretation of the First Amendment. He maintained an absolute separation between religion and government which unfortunately, became widely accepted because it agreed with popular sentiment — not with the First Amendment. Justice Black maintained that this program would fall squarely under his understanding of the First Amendment. The lone dissenter in the case was Justice Stanley Reed.[16] Reed maintained that there had been no "establishment of religion and that First Amendment does not forbid 'every friendly gesture between church and state.'" In his opinion, "...devotion to the great principle of religious liberty should not lead us into a rigid interpretation of the constitutionality guarantee which conflicts with religious habits of our people." But Justice Black won again. He argued that the McCollum Case was clearly forbidden by the First Amendment, of course, as re-written and interpreted by Justice Black.

One of the aspirations the Catholic community cherished when the appeal to the Supreme Court was decided as the path to pursue was freedom from community prejudice. There is, after all, a clear distinction between the interpretation of a law and its constitutionality and what the people think about the subject involved. Catholics understood that they were not going to win any popularity contest. From the beginning their schools had been black-balled by Horace Mann. Interpreting the Constitution, however, was another matter. Certainly public prejudice would not interfere at this point, they assumed, and certainly the Justices of the Supreme Court would not be guilty of such human weaknesses when they interpreted the meaning of the Constitution. How wrong they were. From the beginning of this case there was such an outpouring of hatred and vitriolic language against the Catholic Church and its schools that it is even difficult to imagine. Highly organized civic and fraternal organizations well known in the local and general communities, neighbors of Catholic parents and children, committed the gravest obscenities to prejudice the outcome of these Cases.

Nothing makes the point as clearly as a little discussion recorded in the Court Record between Justice Frankfurter and Attorney Franklin. Franklin was the lawyer representing the appellees in the McCollum Case. In an exchange between Justice Frankfurter and Attorney Franklin, the following insight into the process occurs.

Justice Frankfurter: The question is whether any kind of scheme which introduced religious teaching into the public school system is the kind of thing we should have in our democratic institutions.

Attorney Franklin: That is a proper question to ask. May I ask, though, that you depend to some extent on the record in this case for what is the proven result of this program. Variations of this program are in effect in at least one thousand school districts in forty-six states, and there is nothing in this record or any actual facts pointed out in the briefs of the friends of the court to support the proposition—

Justice Frankfurter: You have a half dozen religious groups opposing this as offensive.

Justice Frankfurter: The very fact you raised this question shows that this kind of thing projects the public schools into religious controversy. What I am saying is that we have these briefs by the religious bodies. We can't go behind them. They purport to speak for those sects.

Attorney Franklin: May I ask you to consider only the law in those briefs and not consider them a supplement to the record?[17]

Attorney Franklin made the point that the business of the Supreme Court was to determine the constitutionality of the statute and not its public popularity. This brief section in the McCollum Record demonstrates that the Justices were concerned about more than the constitutionailty of the statute which they were to interpret. The Supreme Court should avoid this kind of intervention if the interpretation of the constitutionality is to be accurate.

As Justice Reed said so memorably, "… a rule of law should not be drawn from a figure of speech."

THE ZORACH CASE

Only a few years after the McCollum decision a similar case occurred in New York City, the Zorach Case of 1952.[18] Different from the McCollum Case in that it allowed released time for those students who wanted to leave "Black's public school," go off the property and attend religion classes, the Supreme Court upheld its constitutionality and, fortunately, Justice William Douglas used the occasion to bring the Supreme Court a breath back toward its pre-Justice Black days in the matter of relations between religion and government.

Douglas therefore rejected absolute separation, pointed out that if there was absolute separation "...the State and religion would be aliens to each other — hostile, suspicious, and even unfriendly." He then cites a number of daily services which would have to cease: Churches could be required to pay property taxes, municipalities would not be able to render fire protection to religious groups...no prayers in our Legislative Halls; appeals to the Almighty in the messages of the Chief Executive; the proclamation making Thanksgiving a holiday, etc." He spoke these particularly memorable words:

"We are a religious people whose institutions presuppose a Supreme Being. We guarantee the freedom to worship as one chooses. We make room for a wide variety of beliefs and creeds as the spiritual needs of man deem necessary. We sponsor an attitude on the part of government that shows no partiality to no one group and that lets each flourish according to the zeal of its adherents and the appeal of its dogma. When the State encourages religious instruction or cooperates with religious authorities by adjusting the schedule of public events to sectarian needs, it follows the best of our traditions. For it then respects the religious nature of our people and accommodates the public service to their spiritual needs. To hold that it may not, would be to find in the Constitution a requirement that the government shows a callous indifference to religious groups. *That would be preferring those who believe in no religion over those who do believe in religion."* [Italics added.]

Justice Douglas moved the Court from the absolutism established by the Everson Case and confirmed by the McCollum Case. Justice Douglas clearly rejects the absolute separatism of Justice Black's position. As the remainder of his statement indicates, the "wall of separation" is left standing. While Douglas abandons Justice Black's severe and ludicrous rhetoric he seems to be saying that it is not necessary to be so uncivil to administer the coup de grace. Read on!

"Government may not finance religious groups nor undertake religious instruction, nor blend secular and sectarian education or use secular institutions to force some or any religion on any person. But we find no constitutional requirement which makes it necessary for government to be hostile to religion and to throw its weight to efforts to widen the effective scope of religious influence."[19]

Thus the ship of state, as far as its relationship with religion, was regaining a mite of its proper balance, thanks to Justice Douglas. In light of Douglas' comment, the future could be one of cooperation and not collision between the government and religion.

The damage Justice Black committed in the Everson and McCollum Cases was not undone. Justice Black had perhaps forever, it seems, undermined the true meaning of the First Amendment. He, Justice Rutledge, and Justice Frankfurter had made the First Amendment read exactly as they wanted it to read and unfortunately exactly as the anti-Catholic, anti-religious forces have wanted it to read for the previous one hundred years plus. The real conflict between Catholicism and the bigotry of people in the New World was not overlooked by the Court. As a thorough reading of O'Neill will illustrate, even some of the other Justices were deeply influenced by the prejudicial approach to the Catholic issue.

NOTES

1) Pierce v. Society of Sisters, 268, U.S. 510 (1925).

2) ibid.

3) Catholic Encyclopedia, Vol. 13, 302-3.

4) Cochran v. Board of Education, 281, U.S. 370 (1929).

5) Public Law, Chapter 281, Section 2-Section 4 (1946).

6) Bill of Rights, Article I (1789).

7) Federal Constitution, Article VI, Section 3 (1789).

8) O'Neill, J. M., *Religion and Education Under the Constitution* New York: Harper and Brothers, 1949), 35.

9) ibid., 9, 10.

10) Everson v. Board of Education, 330, U.S. 1 (1947).

11) O'Neill, 66 ff.

12) ibid., 78 ff. O'Neill adds this significant paragraph: "...he was addressing the Representatives of the Danbury, Connecticut, Baptists, who at that time, and for years afterward, did not enjoy a status of full religious liberty and equality. The established Congregational Church of Connecticut had preferred status. No other religious group had equal rights with the Congregationalists in Connecticut until 1818 and for years after that only other Christian denominations! Certainly the Baptists of Connecticut knew this. Moreover, the fact that Jefferson knew it is attested by his rather bitter references to the New England Congregationalists in his discussions of civil and religious freedom. Even today the Constitution of Connecticut provides: "Each and every society or denomination of Christians in this state shall have and enjoy the same and equal powers, rights, and privileges...." This situation was remedied in 1843 by an extreme example of judicial legislation when the Supreme Court of Connecticut in doing the right thing in the wrong way, decided (with magnificent disregard for the meaning of language and the intent of constitution makers) that "Christians" meant "any religious group or organization." (p. 83)

13) ibid., 204 ff.

14) ibid., 208.

15) McCollum v. Board of Education, 333, U.S. 203 (1948)

16) O'Neill, 244 ff.

17) ibid., 234.

18) Zorach v. Clauson, 343, U.S. 306 (1952)

19) ibid., Section 313-314

CHAPTER 9

Supreme Court Decisions — Part B

Many assumed that the "problem" of religion and religious education had been cleaned up around the turn of the century. Legislation in various States would certainly have eliminated any remnants of religious instruction, worship, or practices in the public schools. Unfortunately the educational powers did not correctly estimate the involvement of schools and even students with religion. Both religious instructions and practices existed in many public schools throughout the nation, especially, it is said, in the South. Strangely enough, just as the deciding battle between the States took place at Gettysburg, the State of Pennsylvania would again be the scene of the Supreme Court's battleground to eliminate this problem of religion in the public schools. Careful study revealed that many schools had retained the practice of opening the day with a scripture reading and the recitation of the Protestant "Our Father." One can only imagine what the Supreme Court would think about this situation.

THE SCHEMPP CASE (June 1963)[1]
The Schempp family, a husband, wife and two of their children, brought suit against Abington Township School District maintaining that religious practices violated the Constitution. Suit was brought against the School District and its officers, including the Superintendent of Public Instruction of the Commonwealth, to enjoin the district from continuing such readings of the Bible and recitation of the Lord's Prayer in public schools. The district court held that the statute was in violation of the First Amendment. The district and superintendent appealed to the Supreme Court. The Court absolutely prohibited any prayers or any form of religious instruction in the public schools, holding by an overwhelming majority of eight to one that the legislation which enabled such actions was invalid.

The only Justice to uphold the practice of prayer in the public schools was Justice Stewart.

Justice Clark delivered the opinion of the Court. Needless to say, he carefully read the history of the question beginning with the Everson Case, reciting the role of all the famous Justices involved. After study of the history of the Supreme Court and the First Amendment, Justice Clark ordered that the statute permitting prayer and the reading of the Bible in the public schools is invalid. Seven other Justices concurred. Justice Stewart alone dissented from the decision. His upholding of the statute was an important historical moment in the history of public and religious education.

Anyone who tries to keep abreast of the daily news must be moved by the extraordinary efforts made by some students, especially twelfth grade graduates, to sabotage their own graduation ceremony by smuggling in a student-made baccalaureate service or even a simple prayer. Somehow it seems the human heart wants to make it known that there is a God and He should be acknowledged and worshipped even in an unplanned way at important moments of life.

In the Schempp Case, decided by the Supreme Court in 1963, all remnants of religion and religious education were unceremoniously banned by the Court.[2] On that occasion, the customary reading of ten verses of Scripture and the recitation of the Lord's Prayer were barred from the nation's public schools. Some found in this sad state of affairs a glimmer of hope in Mr. Justice Stewart's affirming the continuance of the scripture and the prayer practice in the public schools.[3] Stewart writes: "It is, I think, a fallacious over-simplification to regard these two provisions as establishing a single constitutional standard of 'separation of Church and State' which can be mechanically applied in every case to delineate the required boundaries between government and religion." He goes on to say "...religion and government must necessarily interact in countless ways." He cites the single example of the chaplains in the armed forces who are paid by federal funds. O'Neill also cites countless other examples of cooperation between the government and religion.

Justice Black's distortion of the meaning of the First Amendment has caused a severe setback for those who wish to find in the First Amendment the hope due parents in the area of religion and education. It should not surprise anyone that in rejecting the public school prayers, Everson received special attention and the cast from that case was prominently mentioned.

Justice Stewart went on to say "...if religious exercises were held to be an impermissible activity in schools, religion is placed at an artificial and state-created disadvantage and a refusal to permit religious exercises thus is seen, not as the realization of state neutrality, but rather as the establishment of a religion of secularism or at the least as government support of the beliefs of those who think that religious exercises should be held only in private."

The following paragraph of Justice Stewart is one to reflect on seriously:
"What seems to me to be of paramount importance, then, is recognition of the fact that the claim advanced here in favor of Bible reading is sufficiently substantial to make simple reference to the constitutional phrase 'establishment of religion' as adequate an analysis of the case before us as the ritualistic invocation of the non-constitutional phrase "separation of Church and State." [Emphasis added.][4]

The importance of the misinterpretation given by Justices Black, Rutledge, Frankfurter had a tremendous influence on everything the Supreme Court subsequently did. No First Amendment issues can escape the spurious demands which these members of the Court imposed on the First Amendment. To give a better understanding of the serious consequence of their actions a few of the subsequent cases, particularly those regarding education, will be examined briefly.

THE ALLEN CASE (June 1968)[5]
New York State passed a statute permitting the purchase and loan of textbooks by all school districts to students enrolled in grades 7 through 12, in the parochial schools as well as in the public and private schools. The Supreme Court of New York State declared the statute unconstitutional. Subsequently it was appealed to the United States Supreme Court and the decision was reversed. The opinion of the Court was presented by Justice White. Quoting the Everson Case, Justice White pointed out that there had to "be a secular legislative purpose and a primary effect that neither advances nor inhibits religion." This was, however, not a unanimous decision. The vote was five affirming the validity of the Statute and four in opposition.

To be sure, Justice Black dissented, using his own words to affirm his opposition: "I believe the New York law held valid is a flat, flagrant, open violation of the First and Fourteenth Amendments which together forbid Congress or State Legislatures to enact any law 'respecting an establishment of religion.'" He goes on to further support his opinion by his spurious application of Jefferson's famous quotation that the First Amendment was intended "to erect a wall of separation between Church and State." In his own memorable words he says "the Everson and McCollum Cases plainly interpret the First and Fourteenth Amendments [those cases have no connection with the Fourteenth Amendment, another example of Black's theory of wishful evolution applied to his decisions] as protecting the taxpayer of a State from being compelled to pay taxes to their government to support the agencies of private religious organizations that taxpayers oppose." (This is his real motive.)

Justice Black, as a parting remark, writes: "And I still believe that the only way to protect minority religious groups from majority religious groups in this country is to keep the wall of separation between Church and State high and impregnable as the First and Fourteenth provide. The Court's affirmation here bodes nothing but evil to religious peace in this country."

The point, however, is that even though the statute was approved by the Supreme Court by a margin of one vote, the Justice Black-Rutledge-Frankfurter opinion lingers on and gathers new myths and greater strength. Indeed it continues to be the most distorted yet compelling and influential educational interpretation of law made in this century.

THE WALZ CASE (May 1970)[6]

A property owner in New York requested the New York Court to enforce an injunction preventing the City Tax Commission from granting property tax exemption to religious organizations for property used only for worship. The tax exemption was affirmed when Justice Douglas gave the opinion of the Court. Interestingly enough he describes the First Amendment in his introduction using these words: "The general principle deducible from the First Amendment... by the Court is this: that we will not tolerate either governmental established religion or governmental interference with religion." He goes on to state that: "short of these expressly proscribed governmental acts there is room for play in the joints productive of a benevolent neutrality which will permit religious exercise to exist without sponsorship and without interference." Douglas also says here that the legislative purpose of property tax exemption is neither the advancement nor the inhibition of religion; it is neither sponsorship nor hostility.[7]

Aside from some interesting history on tax exemption, Justice Douglas notes that "separation in this context cannot mean the absence of all contact."

In the Walz Case, Justice Brennan (of later Roe-Wade fame) concurs. He, as we learn later, develops into the Court's absolutist as far as the First Amendment and religious education are concerned. In a real way, even while concurring in the opinion that tax exemption is legal, he at the same time sets the ground work for his own future prejudicial opinions about favorable education statutes.

Typically, Justice Brennan takes time in his written opinions to give a lengthy history of the question before the Court. In this instance he begins with the story of Thomas Jefferson, who during his presidency granted tax exemption to the Washington Churches. He further points out that James Madison was present at sessions of the Virginia General Assembly that voted for exemptions in that Commonwealth. "The more longstanding and widely accepted a practice, the greater its impact on constitutional interpretation. History is particularly compelling in the present case because of the undeviating acceptance given religious tax exemptions in our earliest days as a nation." Brennan goes on to say that such overwhelming historical support permits no question about affirming a favorable tax exemption decision.

After his thorough survey of the history, purpose, and operation of religious tax exemptions, Brennan concludes "...the exemptions do not serve the essentially religious activities of religious institutions. Their principal effect is to carry out secular purposes — the encouragement of public service activity and of pluralistic society." This he considers to be a benefit to the community and that all Churches by their existence contribute to the diversity of association viewpoint and enterprise so highly valued by all.

One can detect, or at least suspect, a tendency (very spotty) of the Supreme Court to be more understanding about the relationship between government and religion. Nevertheless, the policy of Black is still evident. The two-pronged test of validity is definitely a creature of the Everson-McCollum Case and not of the Constitution.

THE LEMON-KURTZMAN/DiCENSO CASES (June 1971)[8]
What inspired these two different cases to arrive at the Supreme Court at the same time is of course impossible to say, Some attribute this to the fatigue of the non-public school clientele. Their waiting for help had become a way of life. The choice they had made to trust in the decision of the Supreme Court was, thus far, in vain. The Court's personnel frequently changed, creating the hope of those who were trying to look after the interest of the non-public schools that such changes might benefit their cause. The non-public-school parents of both Rhode Island and Pennsylvania were working for the passage of legislation which would be helpful to the survival of their non-public schools.

The Rhode Island Case or DiCenso Case concerned a teacher's salary supplement of not more than fifteen percent of an eligible current teacher's pay. The law stipulated that the teacher must offer only those "subjects which are taught in the public schools of the State, be properly certified, and use teaching materials available in the public schools. Such teachers would be eligible only if they agreed in writing not to teach religion as long as they received State supplements to their salary.

The Pennsylvania Law requested that the State purchase secular educational services such as teacher's salaries, textbooks, and educational materials. The reimbursement for these services could be made only for courses in four subject areas: mathematics, modern foreign language, physical science, and physical education. Any subject "expressing religious teaching or the morals or forms of worship" would be prohibited. Standardized tests approved by the Superintendent of Public Instruction would evaluate the results.

Justice Douglas wrote the opinion of the Court that both "statutory schemes" were unconstitutional. In previous First Amendment school cases two reasons were cited as a constitutional test: there must be a secular legislative purpose and a primary effect that neither advances nor inhibits religion. By the way, those two purposes come from the Everson and McCollum Cases authored by Justice Black, who had joined Justice Douglas in this present negative decision. Justice Douglas in his opinion borrowed from the Walz Case, which approved tax exemption for church property. In that Case the Court had mentioned that the legal tests mentioned above did not eliminate the problem. What must also be assured, he said, quoting Walz, is that there is no excessive government entanglement. Thus, he created a third test.

In both these cases the Court declared that the supervision or surveillance of these programs would entail an excess of government involvement. Also mentioned was that one must begin examining these two different cases by recognizing the nature of the parochial schools. According to the authors of the decision, the essence of parochial schools is the propagation of the religious faith. They point out that "they (parochial schools) came into existence because Protestant groups were perverting the public schools by using them to propagate their faith." The decision went on to indicate that other dissenting sects established their own schools — Lutherans, Methodists, Presbyterians, and others. "The constitutional right of dissenters to substitute their own parochial school for public schools was sustained by the Court in Pierce v. Society of Sisters." This interpretation of Pierce v. Society of Sisters is very limiting and misleading.

The decision hangs heavily on the new ingredient identified in Douglas' decision. The question of surveillance required by these new programs would be what the Court has labeled as invalid, namely, excessive entanglement. The Court admits that there is already surveillance over sectarian schools, but such is necessary only to meet minimum educational standards. As the decision puts it, they have never faced "the problem of policing sectarian schools." Justice Douglas mentions in his decision, with which Justice Black concurs, that "whatever might be the result in case of grants to students, it is clear that once one of the States finances a private school it is duty bound to make certain that the school stays within secular bounds and does not use the public funds to promote sectarian causes." That is what the First Amendment is all about, according to Justice Black. To prove his point, he lifted a metaphor from Thomas Jefferson's letter to the Baptist Conference that stated there must be "a wall of separation" between Church and State.

In interpreting the First Amendment, Justice Black not only gave that particular reason to govern valid relationships between Church and religion, but he helped create this new test. Excessive entanglement could not be tolerated and he quoted Madison's statement "three pence only" to indicate there should be no financial involvement between Church and State. Again, another of Black's indiscriminate uses of history.

In both the Lemon case and the DiCenso case, legislation which gave great promise of substantial assistance to non-public schools was thus declared unconstitutional. This decision, said the Court, was made for the good of the parochial schools because the law would place "the State astride a sectarian school and give it power to dictate what is or is not secular."

Numerous quotations about the danger of destroying the purpose of the parochial school, and long quotations from the Catholic Schools Superintendent's Handbook in Rhode Island, indicate the obvious fact that the schools in question are indeed religious. The case ends with a quotation from (where else?) Everson: "No tax in any amount, large or small, can be levied to support any religious activates or institutions whatever they may be called or whatever form they may adopt to teach religion." In conclusion Justice Douglas, supported by Justice Black, adds: "We reiterated the same idea in Zorach, McGowen, Torcaso and [our ever dependable and reliable] McCollum Case." Indeed they did!

In this decision, the Court points out the ways which these religious school matters are handled in various nations. Moslem nations, Sweden, Newfoundland,

Ireland, England, for example, have a long history of financing sectarian education. These nations control the schools by prescribed standards and allow non-denominational membership on the Board of Directors. This deserves some study and careful consideration by those in charge of American education.

Justice Brennan also submits a negative decision in these cases. Brennan points out in a footnote that for similar reasons he is opposed to the Tilton Case which was also being considered about the same time.

Justice Brennan has his own test for determining, as he puts it, what the Framers meant to foreclose on and what our (Court's) decisions on an establishment clause have forbidden. Do those statutes before the court a) serve the essentially religious activities of religious institutions; b) employ the organs of government for essentially religious purposes; c) use essentially religious means to serve governmental ends where secular means would suffice? He then tests the Lemmon and DiCenso cases, according to his own new test. Brennan misses being *the* absolutist in the Supreme Court by a number of years and by the absence of some catchy metaphor which he could misinterpret. The conclusion comes out the same. Brennan is opposed, absolutely, to every form of aid to non-public schools. He carefully reviews the terrible history of religious division and deeply fears that non-believers may not be the greatest difficulty. He fears most the secularization of a creed which becomes involved and dependent upon government. He also points out another problem. When a sectarian institution accepts financial aid it becomes obligated under the Fourteenth Amendment not to discriminate in admission policies and faculty selections. Brennan summarizes his position in these words: "The symbolism of tax exemption is significant as a manifestation and organized religion is not expected to support the State; by the same token the State is not expected to support the Church." This statement could be challenged. Religion supports the State in many ways.

Justice Brennan makes the following observation: "But I do not read Pierce or Allen (both cases he supported vigorously) as supporting the proposition that public subsidy of sectarian institutions' secular training is permissible in state training. I read them as supporting the proposition that as an identifiable set of skills and an identifiable quantum of knowledge, secular education may be effectively provided either in the religious context of parochial schools or outside the context of religion in public schools." Both Pierce and Allen have been interpreted in quite a different sense. Do not both cases tell us something about the responsibility and "high duty of those who nurture" the child — the parents, a word seldom used either in public school literature or Court decisions?

THE TILTON CASE (June 1971)[9]

This statute provided for construction grants for colleges and universities. Its single limitation was that the government retained a twenty year concern in any facility constructed under the Act. After the twenty year period, the college would be the sole owner and free to use the building in any way it saw fit. A common objection was that the recipients were sectarian and therefore the buildings would be eligible to be used for the teaching of religion after twenty years.

The Act was declared constitutional except for that portion providing the twenty year limitation on the religious use of facilities constructed with federal funds.

One of the most important dicta in this decision was the great compliment paid the sectarian colleges by a comparison made to the Lemmon v Kurtzman Case: "There is less danger here than in Church related primary and secondary schools dealing with impressionable children that religion will permeate the area of secular education, since religious indoctrination is not a substantial purpose or activity of these church related colleges." This interesting comment is something that all religious educators should reflect on. The question raised at this point is whether or not the statement is true. The fact is that very many Catholic Colleges do indeed conduct programs of evangelization. These are substantial purposes and activities at many Catholic institutions.

It should be noted that Justice Brennan filed a dissenting opinion.

THE NYQUIST CASE (June 25, 1973)[10]
This New York education statute contained three specific requests for their non-public elementary and secondary schools. The first request was for direct grants to nonpublic schools for maintenance and repairs for facilities and equipment. Section Two asked for a tuition reimbursement for parents whose children were attending nonpublic schools and whose annual taxable income was less than $5,000. And the third program, which had three parts to it, was designed to give tax relief to parents failing to qualify for tuition reimbursement. At the district level the first and second parts were declared invalid but the third section was held constitutional.

By a vote of six to three however, the Supreme Court ruled that the statute with its three-fold provisions also violated the establishment clause, that it is not sufficiently restricted, and therefore it will have the impermissible effect of advancing sectarian activity in the school. Because, as the Justices concluded, the impermissible effect for advancing religion is so clear, there was no need to use the third reserved weapon, namely, entanglement with religion.

Three Justices dissented from the tax relief to parents section, but they were in the minority: Justices Rehnquist, Berger and White. To put the Nyquist Case in simple language, the Supreme Court affirmed Section one and two of the District Court's decision, and they reversed the District Court on the third Section — the Tax Relief to parents. The entire Statute was held unconstitutional.

CONCLUSION
Special reasons make an examination of these Supreme Court Cases interesting. They all depend to some degree on the famous Justices Black-Rutledge-Frankfurter's interpretation of the First Amendment in the Everson and McCollum Cases. This, in effect, had the force of a new law, and, unfortunately, has been completely and total-

ly unquestioned by other members of the Supreme Court. The interpretaion given in the Everson and McCollum cases, was a surrender to those who hated the Catholic religion and the Catholic schools, a condition which has existed from the very beginning of the Republic.

From the beginning, the Supreme Court determined a simple test: the statute under consideration must have a secular legislative purpose that neither advances nor inhibits religion. If the statute did either of these things, it was held in violation of the First Amendment. In the Lemmon-Kurtzman Case, another prong was added to this famous dual test for validity: there must not be excessive entanglement between government and religion. Justice Brennan, because he got a late start on the Court and was not able to participate in the judgments made on the Everson and McCollum Cases, made his own test in Lemmon-Kurtzman/DiCenso which reads as follows: a) the statute must not serve the essentially religious activities of religious institutions; b) employ the organs of government for essentially religious purposes; c) use essentially religious means to serve governmental ends where secular means would suffice.

Unquestionably, the attorneys representing the non-public school parents and their children have done a superb job. But their power cannot match that of the Justices of the Supreme Court. At one point those plans submitted to the Court are referred to as "great schemes" to get aid. Even the Justices are impressed with the genius of those who figure out how one might get around the Court. It has become like a chess game and each time the Justices are able to checkmate. But the attorneys for the parents cannot change the laws.

It is unlikely that we have among our number anyone with the intelligence to outwit the Justices at this tragic game of financing the education of non-public school children.

Perhaps this is why some of our attorneys have submitted schemes which offered to surrender things that would surely destroy Catholic education. In desperation offers of programs essential for Catholic education have been put on the table. Fortunately, the Justices did see what we did not see. Parents have supported every move that their leaders have urged and they have accepted with great hope every plan which seems to them and to all of us, reasonable and fair solutions to what is not only a non-public-school problem, but indeed a national problem.

Justice Brennan in the Lemon Case observes that Pierce recognized the right of parochial schools to exist because their parents have the right to choose. But he goes on to state that he did not read anything in that decision about supporting them with public subsidy.

I suggest that the members of the Supreme Court, just after saying their night prayers and before going to bed, read over the *underlined* sections above and meditate thoughtfully on these two sentences:

"Congress shall make no law respecting an establishment of religion, or prohibiting the free exercise thereof."

Like Justice Brennan, I cannot read that law as the Justices have.

NOTES

1) Abington Township v. Schempp, 374, U.S. 203 (1963)

2) ibid., 295.

3) ibid., 311 ff.

4) ibid., 311.

5) James E. Allen v. Board of Education, 392, U.S. 236 (1968)

6) Frederick Walz v. Tax Commissioner, New York, 397, U.S. 664 (1967)

7) McConnell, "Harvard Law Review," (Cambridge, Massachusetts: May 1990), 1698.

8) Lemon/Kurtzman-DiCenso, 89, 509, 570, (1971); cf. McConnell, "The Lemon Test in School Aid Cases," 1678 ff.

9) Tilton v. Richardson, 403, U.S. 672 (1971)

10) Committee for Public Education v. Nyquist, 413, U.S. 756 (1973)

CHAPTER 10

Supreme Court Decisions — Part C

This is the third section of Supreme Court cases dealing specifically with non-public education; their major concern is government financial aid for the elementary and secondary levels. It is important that these responses of the highest Court in the land be examined. There is no question that the Catholic population and its Bishops chose to pursue the legal path in an attempt to solve their school problem. Thus a sampling of relevant cases beginning with Pierce (1925) and ending with these current educational decisions of the Supreme Court has been listed and examined. Whether or not United States Catholics made a wise choice in pursuing the legal path to what they hoped would be justice remains as yet undetermined.

CATHEDRAL ACADEMY CASE (June 25, 1973)[1]
New York State mandated a statute making certain payments from public funds to non-public religious schools for some testing and record keeping. The Court ruled this unconstitutional aid to religion where the aid for secular functions is not identifiable and separable from aid from sectarian activities. Eight favored the decision but Justice White dissented. The Court maintained that it was only "fanciful" thinking that a State could reimburse church related schools for costs incurred in performing any services mandated by State Law. It is interesting to note that Justices Douglas, Brennan, and Marshall maintained that the decision was already made that very day in the Nyquist decision. Justice White dissented from the opinion of the Court and his opinion is very interesting and should be noted: "…the Court continues to misconstrue the First Amendment in a manner that discriminates against religion and is contrary to the fundamental educational needs of the country…"

McNAIR CASE (June 25, 1973)[2]
This case concerned a statutory plan for aiding colleges by issuance of revenue bonds for projects which excluded sectarian study or religious worship. The South Carolina State authority would lease back the facilities and recover payment of bonds. The Supreme Court upheld the proposal although three Justices dissented: Brennan,

Douglas, and Marshall. These three agreed that the scheme involved the State in an unconstitutional program because it required policing college affairs and therefore violated the First Amendment.

MEEK-PITTENGER CASE (May, 1975)[3]

A Pennsylvania statute provided textbooks and workbook materials on loan and certain auxiliary services. The statute included, beside the textbook loan, certain instructional materials (charts, films, etc.), professional staff, and supporting materials to provide services required for remedial and accelerated programs, guidance and testing, speech and hearing, to qualified non-public parochial school students. All these services are, of course, available in the public schools.

The Court upheld only the textbook loan provision. It was ruled that the other requests in the statute violated the First Amendment. Justices Brennan, Douglas, and Marshall expressed the view that the textbook loan provision of the statute was also unconstitutional because the entire program advanced the cause of religion.

Most interesting in this Case was the opinion expressed by Chief Justice Berger. He upheld the textbook loan program but dissented from the Court's decision that the other programs violated the First Amendment. He indicated that denying such auxiliary services would penalize children because of their parents' choice of religious exercise thus "denying equal protection" to the children in religious schools and improperly applying the religion clause of the First Amendment to discriminate against religious activities. By the way, both Justices Rehnquist and White also dissented along with the Chief Justice. They did not support the Court's deciding that instructional material and equipment, as well as auxiliary services involving public school personnel, were unconstitutional. Nevertheless, only the textbook section of this Law survived.

ROEMER, III CASE (June, 1976)[4]

A Maryland statute providing state non-categorical grants to accredited private colleges including religious affiliated institutions (except seminaries or those granting theological degrees) was approved as constitutional by the Court in a six to three vote. Justice Brennan, however, maintained that the First Amendment prohibited such subsidies to church affiliated colleges because this benefited religion and advanced it. Justice Marshall joined him in this dissent and Justice Stewart dissented because the college theology courses were devoted to deepening religious experience rather than teaching theology as an academic discipline. The Statute was declared valid.

WOLMAN-WALTER CASE (June, 1977)[5]

The Wolman-Walter case concerned an Ohio State statute to provide non-public elementary and secondary schools with secular textbooks on loan; standardized tests and scoring services as used in the public schools; diagnostic and therapeutic services to students; field trips, instructional materials, and equipment for students. The statute was considered to be constitutional with the exception of the public monies used for instructional materials and equipment for students and for transportation (field trips).

MUELLER-NOYES/ALLEN CASE (June, 1983)[6]

In Minnesota a number of parents took advantage of tax deductions for expenses incurred in sending their children to parochial school. The Court held that to deduct tuition, textbooks, and transportation did not violate the First Amendment. Five of the Justices upheld the decision noting that the deduction was available for children attending public, non-sectarian private schools as well as parochial schools. Four Justices (Marshall, Brennan, Blackman, Stevens) dissented, maintaining that the prohibitions of the First Amendment include tax benefits as well as subsidies of other kinds.

AGUILAR-FELTON CASE (July 1, 1985)[7]

In 1966 the city of New York provided (NDEA) Title I Program Instructional Services to parochial school students on the premises of parochial schools. These included remedial reading, reading skills, remedial mathematics, English as a second language, and guidance services. The programs were conducted by regular public school employees and were held in parochial school classrooms. Taxpayers challenged this practice, alleging that this Title I Program violated the establishment clause.

Five of the Justices led by Brennan stated that the First Amendment bars the use of federal funds to send public school teachers and other professionals into religious schools to carry on instruction or to provide clinical service.

Chief Justice Berger dissented, noting that the programs being offered were necessary to provide essential educational services to the children and "imposed no real threat of creating an established church." Justice White also dissented, expressing the view that the programs were valid and were not prohibited by the First Amendment. Justice Rehnquist dissented for similar reasons. Justice O'Connor joined in part with Rehnquist, stating that the establishment clause decisions have not barred remedial assistance to parochial school children but rather remedial assistance on the premises of the parochial school. Justice O'Connor went on to say that the Case did not violate the "effects test" nor the "entanglement" clause and that the decision which the Court was reaching would deprive many school children of vital educational services. It was in this context that she mentioned the possible use of a portable classroom near the school. Justice O'Connor stated that this ruling by the Court (5 to 4 against) "does not spell the end of the Title I Program...impoverished children who attend parochial schools may also continue to benefit...possibly in portable classrooms. Where these are not economically and logistically feasible the children will suffer and for them "the Court's decision is tragic."

GRAND RAPIDS-BALL CASE (July, 1985)[8]

In Michigan supplementary classes for students in non-public schools, primarily sectarian, were financed by the public schools, taught by teachers hired by the public schools but conducted in non-public school classrooms leased by the public schools. Signs were placed on the rooms identifying them as public school classes while in session. This was considered a shared-time program.

Five of the Justices held that both the shared-time program and the community education program were impermissible. Four of the Justices concurred only in part or dissented totally from the opinion. Chief Justice Berger held that the community education program was in violation of the First Amendment but this was not true of the shared-time program. Justice O'Connor held the shared-time program did not advance religion but the community education Program tended to do so. Justice White maintained that the programs in question were well within the authority of the States and were not forbidden by the establishment clause. Justice Renhquist also dissented. The Statute, however, was struck down.

SERVICES FOR THE BLIND CASE (March, 1986)[9]

A blind student applied to the Washington State Commission for aid to continue his biblical studies at a Christian College. The Washington Supreme Court upheld the denial made because they concurred that this request for assistance violated the First Amendment. Justice Marshall, however, held that extending assistance under the State Vocational Rehabilitation Program to a blind person who chose to study at a Christian College to become a pastor or minister was not precluded by the First Amendment. All nine Justices voted in favor of this decision.

ZOBREST CASE (June, 1993)[10]

The parents of a deaf student requested a sign language interpreter to accompany him to classes in a Catholic high school. At the Arizona State level it was held that such a request was contrary to the federal constitution. The Supreme Court in a five to four decision upheld that such relief was not barred by the establishment clause. A sign language interpreter would neither add to nor subtract from the school's sectarian environment. Justice Blackman, with Justices Souter, Stevens and O'Connor, maintained that the constitutional question should not have been introduced because as Blackman stated, the establishment of religion clause is violated by placement in a parochial school classroom, a public school employee whose duty, as in the present case, consists of relaying religious messages.

The Court approved the request.

AGOSTINI-FELTON CASE (June, 1997)[11]

This case is a re-evaluation of the 1985 AGUILAR-FELTON CASE heard by the Supreme Court in 1985 (cf. above). At that time the Court decided that the benefits coming to parochial school students under Title I NDEA were valid, but they could not be provided by public school teachers paid by federal funds who entered the parochial school to provide these services. Involved were thousands of parochial school children who qualified under the stipulations of Title 1. This program included remedial Reading, Reading Skills, Remedial Mathematics, English as a second language and Guidance Services. The original case, cited above, was defeated by a 5 to 4 decision and classes for parochial school students were moved from the classrooms in parochial schools to mobile units or portable classrooms nearby the schools.

At that time Chief Justice Berger saw no threat to the First Amendment in the existing practice. Justices White and Renhquist also dissented from the majority for similar reasons. Justice O'Connor was very clear and held that the practice did not violate the "effects test" nor, she wrote, did it involve "entanglement." Moreover, Justice O'Connor stated that the service provided was necessary.

In the present decision Justice O'Connor said that the establishment clause has "significantly changed" since the 1985 case. Her reasoning was basically the same as given above in the Felton Case: the practice "does not run afoul of the three primary criteria we currently use to evaluate whether government aid has the effect of advancing religion." Justice O'Connor continues, "We therefore hold that a federally funded program providing supplementary aid, remedial instruction to disadvantaged children on a neutral basis, is not invalid under the establishment clause when such instruction is given on the premises of sectarian schools when the instruction is given by government employees…"

By a five to four decision the Court overturned its 1985 decision which required that such programs were to be conducted off the site of parochial and other non-public schools. One writer headlines the story by stating that "those vans and trailers parked outside Catholic elementary schools soon may disappear…" This decision, a significant about face by the Supreme Court, was made by Justices O'Connor, Rehnquist, Scalia, Kennedy, and Thomas, Jr.

This decision also overturned that part of School District of Grand Rapids v. Ball (cf. above) that considered the validity of "Shared Time" at public expense to students in non-public schools.

REFLECTIONS ON CONSTITUTIONAL RESPONSES TO EDUCATION
(1925 to present)
One might approach an evaluation of the legal relationship between the State and religion during these past 70 years in many ways. Although reluctant to evaluate the work of the Supreme Court, honor requires such an attempt. Reading the responses of the Supreme Court during these past 70 years is like reading the Book of the Apocalypse.

Interpretations of that Holy Book abound. I like to think of the Book of Apocalypse as a kind of insight into the history of the Church from about the year 100 to the end of the world. What it says to me is that the Church will have its ups and downs, its glories and sorrows, its advances and setbacks. What we must expect according to the writing of the prophet John is that the Church will go through a joy-sorrow cycle. There will be days of happiness; there will also be days of crisis and hopelessness; in the end the Church will prevail. Again, I repeat, this is only a very personal interpretation of that complicated book by the great prophet John.

In a way, that explanation of the Church's joy-sorrow cycle as seen in the Apocalypse seems to reflect the history of our religion-state relationship these past 70 years. Although religious beliefs seem to peak at a given moment, this period precedes a depressing and negative response. One cannot help but notice this pattern in the fate of religious schools in these cases. Exhilaration after the Pierce Decision, when certainly the religious school experience was one of great happiness and satisfaction, was soon followed by the disastrous Everson and McCollunr Cases where the greatest possible handicaps were created for religious education: the absolutism of Justice Black; the ramblings of Justice Rutledge; the effects of public prejudices on Justice Frankfurter's interpretation of the constitutional question. Then came a brief period of promise and hope, especially as one reads Justice Douglas' opening words in the Zorach Case (1952), and the extraordinary statements of Justice Stewart in the Schempp Case (1963). One could not help but feel that a new era was not far away. The Court seemed to be saying that the absolutism of the 40s was not the way to settle church-state issues and that a more intelligent and understanding approach was required by the true understanding of the Constitution.

In recent years, when the Courts had to deal with the sensitive case of the blind student and his continued studies at a Christian College to become a minister, and the couching Zobrast Case about the deaf student and his sign language interpreter, one feels that the Court must have accidentally stumbled upon the Sermon on the Mount.

One cannot help noticing that in the meantime, even though there have been many changes in the personnel of the Court, Justice Brennan succeeded in emerging as the absolutist as well as an exact clone of Justice Black. Absolutism continues for the time in the thinking of the Court. The statement of Chief Justice Berger's opinion in the famous Aguilar-Felton Case (1985) when he dissented from the decision of the Court regarding public school personnel going into parochial schools for remedial instruction and guidance, should be kept in mind by the Justices and all: this Case, he wrote "imposed no real threat of creating an established Church."

This lack of threat, of course, is the issue. This was the issue that the Court was supposed to deal with in the Everson and McCollum Cases; this is the issue that must be dealt with in every church-state issue considered on the basis of the First Amendment. Does this statute impose a real threat of creating an established church? Unfortunately the Court issue is so affected by the frightening prejudice and bigotry surrounding these questions hat it is difficult to separate them for study.

The general lack of understanding of this key question makes the issue raised by Chief Justice Berger extremely important. Is there any action threatened or any law proposed that would make any Church the official Church of the nation? No such threat is apparent. The Catholic Church is not interested in becoming the official Church of the nation. The Catholic Church is interested in winning the hearts of the people of the world in so far as possible, and will continue doing that as long as the government rulers of this world do not prevent this. In fact, history shows that even if the princes of this world do stand in its way, the Church will continue its mission. Those who worry about the role of the Church in this world must keep in mind that the Kingdom that Jesus came to establish is not of this world. The Catholic Church makes no threats to any nation in the world; it demands no political service from any individual; it claims no infallibility except over matters of faith and morals; it asks compliance only to the laws of God and just human laws, it asks its people to be good and loyal citizens of God's Kingdom and of their country.

We wonder how our nation could wander so far from the truth given us by our Founding Fathers. The hatred of Catholics that motivated the actions of so many and the long history of hatred and bigotry has already been partially retold in this document. Terrible as it may seem, certain Supreme Court Justices seem to have absorbed some of the bigotry of many people in this nation; at the very least they recognized this bigotry and were moved by what they observed. This has led to the crisis in our times between church and state.

Justice Brennan, who has never proposed himself as a friend of religious education, takes time in his response in the Lemon-Kurtzman/DiCenso cases to point out those nations who do welcome and finance competing educational programs. In his response to that Case he cites the governments of Sweden, Newfoundland, Ireland, England; he fails to mention others such as Canada and most of the emerging nations.

Our national educational program does reasonably well in the family of nations. The rankings on standardized tests show that our public schools are eleventh or twelfth from the top of the list. It would be good if our educational authorities took a careful look at these competing national educational programs and consider the advantage of competition for our educational monopoly. I would recommend that they look into the English, the Irish, and the Canadian programs, for deeper insights into what can be done. I have had the opportunity to personally investigate those three systems of education. They have many advantages. First, I never read or heard of any great conflict between church and state about these educational systems. Secondly, the competition among the different systems is healthy for everyone, especially teachers and students. And finally, I would note that there is no religion divisiveness because of the school programs in the examples cited.

Certainly we should be proud of our public school system. But we are also very proud of our non-public school programs; the Government should be proud as well. It is time that we say and say clearly so there will be no misunderstanding: the non-public schools cannot survive and serve any significant number of youngsters without financial help from the Federal Government. We all look expectantly for someone, some leader, to come along and explain education in such a way that the

Government will embrace all systems, thus respecting parental choice as instructed in Pierce, and raise our educational standards to new and glorious heights.

The last decision cited deserves a special comment. The trailers and vans outside parochial schools since the 1985 decision will soon disappear. Justice O'Connor did a magnificent job in leading the majority to the sanity of the June 1997 educational decision. But as happy as one can be about the cessation of that absurd situation, the words of Justice O'Connor bring us back to reality. She said that the present case "does not run afoul of the three primary criteria we currently use" to evaluate government aid to parochial schools. O'Connor's thinking brings us back to Everson, McCollum and Justices Black, Frankfurter, Rutledge, and Brennan. These cases and these Justices still block clear vision of our national educational aspirations. Justice O'Connor, on the other hand, inspires great hope in those who accept the First Amendment just as it is.

In May 1987 the Harvard Law Review published an entire issue on "Developments in the Law — Religion and the State."[12] One might be inclined to think that the whole three-pronged test of the establishment clause was simply taken for granted — a matter of history accepted and filed away for future use. But such is not the case. The whole question of the Court's position on the Lemon Case and the test which it provoked has, according to this Journal, "…proven problematic." To that very happy and still alive piece of legal information a statement by Justice O'Connor brings an equal amount of joy and hope: "The Lemon test has no more grounding in the history of the First Amendment than does the Wall theory on which it rests."[13]

> "Congress shall make no law respecting an establishment of religion or abridging the free exercise thereof." AMEN

NOTES

1) State of New York v. Cathedral Academy, 434, U.S. 125 (1973)

2) Hunt v. McNair, 413, U.S. 734 (1973)

3) Meek v. Pittenger, 421, U.S. 349 (1975)

4) Roemer v. Board of Public Works, MD., 426, U.S. 736 (1976)

5) Wolman v. Walter, 433, U.S. 229 (1977)

6) Meuller-Noyes v. Allen, 463, U.S. 388 (1983)

7) Aquilar v. Felton, 473, U.S. 402 (1985)

8) Grand Rapids v. Ball, 473, U.S. 373 (1985)

9) Witters v. Washington Department of Blind, 474, U.S. 481 (1986)

10) Zobrest v. Catalina Foothills, 509, U.S. (1993)

11) Agostini v. Felton, 96- 552 (1997)

12) McConnell, *Harvard Law Review,* May 1987, "Developments in the Law — Religion and the State".

The Harvard Law Review of May 1987 has a complete review of the literature regarding the whole question of legal developments on such matters as the Lemon test. For a complete analysis of this important subject cf. part C of the review mentioned above.

13) McConnell, 1727, n.

Miscalculation

My grandfather died when I was in my twenties. He died too soon. I was just getting to know him. My father was crazy about him and used to tell me fascinating stories about what my grandfather did and said. One of the best stories I remember took place at the turn of the century. To be exact, it was New Year's Eve 1899.[1]

My father was eleven years old when his family still lived in Kilcoo, Ireland, a little village in County Down. When pressed hard my father would admit that the family had to leave Ireland because his dad could not make a living there. So they moved to Milam, which is near Birmingham (England), and there the family (mom and dad, three boys, one girl) took up residence. My grandfather was a farmer, and from what I learned, he was pretty good at his trade. In England, however, he had to work in the mines. Apparently he was also rather restless, and as typical of the Irish, he was hopeful. These characteristics may explain in part this story which my father told me.

On New Year's Eve, just as the new century was about to begin, my grandfather had one of his famous family meetings. Everyone marched into the parlor, as it was known in those days, removed the covers from the furniture, sat around a marble table in the middle of the room, and grandfather read to them from the Bible. Then my grandfather gave a little talk that he had apparently been planning for some time. In essence he said, I want my family to know that we are going to move again. This time, as soon as we get enough money, we shall move to the United States. I have been reading about that great country, and I have letters from relatives and friends already in America. From everything I can learn, it must be the most wonderful country in the world. It has such a remarkable record of achievement, that everyone is saying "America is about to enter its Golden Age."

A few years later, the family did move to Western Pennsylvania and settled down in a delightful little town known as New Castle.

My grandfather's predictions that America would experience its Golden Age in the Twentieth Century struck me, and as I grew older I began to discover why he had said such a thing.

Chapter 11 – Miscalculation

The period before 1900 is known to many as the Gay Nineties. There was not another period in the history of our Nation more colorful. It was the time of long rustling dresses, colorful bonnets, stiff collars, and barbershop quartets. To me it will always be the period of some of the most fascinating music and good, decent family entertainment.

More important, America was in the midst of the Industrial Revolution. The great industrial giant had suddenly awakened and was belching out smoke from every stack. Men were working around the clock in the mines that provided coal and gathering other raw materials for the mills that were turning out a wealth of products. It seemed that everyone was working. The American railroad system and rivers were spreading out like giant hands; and along the fingers, trains and vessels rushed back and forth, connecting almost all major cities and towns, delivering from one place raw materials and to another finished products. Thousands of people also traveled to and fro.

The world of science was in the spotlight. The great scientific laboratories of Europe, especially in Leipzig, Rome, Madrid, and London were gradually being recreated in the United States as hundreds of American students finished their studies, returned home and began to develop new labs at the University of Pennsylvania, Catholic University of America, John Hopkins, Berkeley University, and others.

Scientific inventions were common.[2] America was boasting about its telephone, its newly discovered light bulb, and as 1900 approached there was a "new toy" to appear on the scene, one which would change the face of the earth. It was the automobile, which would be followed soon by the airplane.

By the way, our educational scene was exciting. Our schools were involved in a great experiment. They included some of the best colleges and universities in the world, but concentration was, at this time, on elementary and secondary schools, with the intention of providing basic education for all American youth. This would be the first time in history that such an experiment was attempted.

In the field of medicine the situation was also exciting and could be summarized by a statement allegedly made at an AMA convention. At the turn of the century a prominent doctor, in a keynote address, supposedly expressed sympathy to those who would be joining their ranks in the years to come. These new doctors, after the year 1900, would never experience the excitement of discovery, of extending the field of medicine because, as the speaker said, everything important had already been accomplished.

Our government was growing rapidly and was demanding and receiving respect from older nations. The new Republic, the United States of America, with its emphasis on democracy was gaining wide-spread attention and respect.

Diplomats from the United States were welcome at almost every Court in the world. The growing military forces of the young nation were highly regarded. Their good will was sought. Their presence around the world and on the seas was welcomed. Their strength and skill in the art of war and peace were acknowledged and their good intentions were generally accepted.

Such was the scene in the Gay Nineties. No wonder my grandfather said that America was entering a Golden Era. If all these things had been accomplished in the early years of this new nation, what would the twentieth century bring? The more I thought about it the more I appreciated my grandfather's excitement. In fact, it wasn't just my grandfather, but as I gradually learned, the poets, the orators, and the politicians were predicting the same thing. If America could grow and produce as it had in these early years, then the twentieth century in America should be the most creative, the most spectacular, the most wondrous of all centuries and might be compared to the great periods in Roman and Greek history that we call the Golden Ages.

Now today we are in the final days of that century. We have the advantage to be able to look back over the century and recall the events that have taken place to this date. Has America experienced its Golden Era? Has it reached its peak as was expected and hoped for by so many when this century began?

In many ways those predictions came true. That little toy that we call a car has now parlayed itself into an important part of social and economic life throughout the world. Our nation is covered with roads; millions of cars and trucks, carrying people and goods, travel twenty-four hours a day.

The airplane has now come to amazing stature. Today airplanes connect every part of the world. In less than a day one can travel to the most distant parts of the earth. Missiles can do the same thing in minutes. Just a few years ago those airplanes moved an entire army from America to the Middle East and successfully restored peace, at least temporarily. Missiles are routinely accomplishing equally amazing things day after day.

Our communication system would astound even the greatest turn of the century technologist. From our own front room the phone can keep us in touch with almost anyone in the world. Through radio and television, we cannot only hear people from other parts of the world, but we can see them. "What [indeed] hath God wrought?"

The wonders of this age are astounding. From the time we rise in the morning to make our coffee, until we go to bed at night and turn on our automatic shutoff radio, each one of us lives in a push-button world.

In every field of endeavor one can see the great progress that has been made. In the world of economics, government, commerce, communications, transportation, medicine, technology and science, America has expanded and grown to such heights that it is difficult to conceive, much less understand. Successfully manned trips to and from the moon have been made and satellites are being sent out routinely to distant planets to study their surface and environment.

One would have to be short-sighted if he did not admit that many of the aspirations and expectations expressed in the Gay Nineties have been realized.

But it is far from a Golden Era. It is not a shangri-la. All kinds of difficulties and problems persist in our world; these we must admit and honestly face.

At least three great depressions and a half dozen recessions have occurred during this past century.

Our nation has existed on the verge of warfare throughout the century. There have been two major wars and several dozen minor ones in the same period of time. It was only a few years ago that the menacing threat of Russian Communism and the Cold War began to abate. For the first time in some 70 years there does not appear to be any imminent threat of war with Russia, nor is there an overwhelming menace posed by communism, at least the Russian version. Yet communism has affected the life of everyone in this nation in one way or another. What Red China has in store for the world remains to be seen.

During the past century the world suffered from the evils of Nazism and experienced wars and events like the Holocaust that are horrible beyond imagination.

Our economic program should be a good one. We are the wealthiest nation in the world. Yet one of every seven people in this country is poor. At this very moment, millions of people are pacing the sidewalks without a job or a decent place to live.

In the meantime, the crime rate has increased over one hundred percent. Over a million men and women, and an ever-increasing number of children, are imprisoned; our major cities report a serious shortage of jails.

The Supreme Court, the highest and most respected court in our Land, in this most advanced civilization, has declared that killing unborn babies is legal, and annually 1.5 million unborn babies are destroyed in this country alone. The horrid practice of partial birth abortion has been approved by the nation's president.

Even though medical knowledge has ballooned, some of the most serious medical problems to face any generation now confront us. The problems of drugs, alcohol, and AIDS are sweeping the country. The ways to avoid these diseases are well known, but we have not been able to convince much less to induce most victims to use the moral cures.

No, it has not been a Golden Age by a long shot. I believe that my grandfather, if he were living, would be able to tell us why it has not been a Golden Era. His answer might go something like this:

America has grown up in almost every conceivable way: militarily, diplomatically, medically, scientifically, technologically, economically; in the arts of communication, government, and even warfare; indeed in every possible way except one. We have failed to let our sense of religion, of moral and spiritual values, develop. Today people approach our problems in a state of almost total ignorance of religious, spiritual, and moral values. Current knowledge is being applied to every conceivable field; but new problems are faced without something that has been part of our culture for centuries: our traditional religious, spiritual, and moral values and beliefs.

Chapter 11 — Miscalculation

It must be admitted that while our nation's growth religiously, morally, and spiritually has been, as a nation, minimal if any, the growth in science and technology has been spectacular. Vatican Council II observed: "No doubt today's progress in science and technology can foster a certain exclusive emphasis on observable data, and an agnosticism about everything else. For the methods of investigations which these sciences use can be wrongly considered as the supreme rule for discovering the whole truth. The danger exists that man confiding too much in modern discoveries may even think that he is sufficient unto himself and no longer seek any higher realities."[3] It is our opinion that this very thing has happened.

In our culture it's axiomatic that the health of any society depends primarily on the health of the families which make it up. The family is the essential unit in our society and it is often said that "as goes the family, thus goes society." There is another part to this axiom. The health of the family depends primarily on the marriage which initiates and creates this basic unit of society.

Marriage is that sacred bond which unites a man and a woman in an indissoluble union through which new life is brought into this world.

If we look at the current situation we must acknowledge the plethora of broken marriages and, therefore, broken families. The real dangers to our society, our culture, and our civilization must-be recognized.

In 1960 there were three marriages for every one divorce. Ten years later the ratio was two marriages for every divorce. Within the last decade there was one divorce for every marriage, and now the number of divorces annually exceeds the number of marriages. The situation continues to deteriorate.

Demographers tell us that to keep our society healthy the average number of children for each mother should be about 2.1 children. This is known as the replacement level for our nation. In 1790 women bore an average of 7.7 children. In the United States birthrates have been below the replacement level for some twenty-five years. Birthrates increased in the eighties but are back down these past few years. For the last decade the fertility rate has been about 1.9.

Our society displays a clear distaste for children. Young married people are very frank about the fact that they want no children — at least until their home is paid for and enough cars and television sets have been acquired. The abortion rate of 1.5 million a year tells us clearly what many think about children. Many simply do not want to be bothered. Daily newspapers carry horrible stories about the mistreatment of infants, children, and even adults. Some babies are killed at the intermission of the school dance by a mother who is still a child herself. The infant's "father" is just looking for a little recreation. More and more one reads of the tragic death of infants conceived and born outside wedlock by mere children who have absolutely no awareness of parental responsibilities. The easiest thing for such young and unprepared "parents" to do is to get rid of such unwanted children before their own life is totally ruined. Far too many people simply look the other way when these devastating tragedies occur as they do more and more frequently these days.

136

These facts also tell us much more about today's families and society:
- the average woman will be living alone by the time she is 50
- the average child has only a 50-50 chance of having a brother or sister
- the average child has a far less than 50-50 chance of having both a brother and sister
- 50 percent of our children live in single parent homes
- 50 percent of our children will grow up without one or both of their real parents[4]

The number of marriages and divorces in our society may shock us, but those who do not marry may shock us more. There are, of course, single, upright men and women who are good people and God-fearing citizens. But there are also a significant number of others who make this sacred union just another form of recreation:
- at least 15 percent of those who "marry" make no commitment — they simply "shack up" as the kids say now
- some men want to "marry" men
- those who engage in indiscriminate sex are principally responsible for one of the devastating diseases of our age: AIDS
- some women want to "marry" women, and some State Governments have encouraged this "union" or "partnership" by recognizing it as legal and provide benefits once reserved for the married only

There are many reasons for the sky-rocketing divorce rate. Certainly the recent emphasis on feminism and the inroads made by gays and lesbians are high on the list of causes. There is room in our society for a feminism which is moderate and sensible in its demands on our culture, but one that rejects motherhood, berates men, and considers child bearing a grave inconvenience if not an insult to their womanhood can hardly be called moderate.

Homosexuality as a lifestyle has again become prominent in society and is extraordinarily widespread.[5] There are an estimated 10 million homosexuals in our society today and 30 percent of them have attempted or will attempt suicide.

Homosexuality, both gays and lesbians, is in many ways a great mystery. Consequently there are an abundance of theories which attempt to explain its nature and causes. Some psychologists maintain that homosexuality is due to genetic causes. "Always Our Children," recently issued by a Committee of the NCCB, as well as a number of other groups and individuals, maintained, among other causes, the condition is genetic. A significant number of respected scientists, however, hold that there is absolutely no reliable proof for such a claim. Homosexualists, some say, hold the genetic theory because it would be an acceptable and respectable answer for gays and lesbians; or because their philosophy of life allows no other possible answer. Likewise this theory provides for some a justification of their own bizarre sexual preferences and behavior.

Many sound scientists maintain that psychological reasons alone underlie the majority of homosexuality cases. There are a few psychologists who suggest that homosexuality is very often the result of a freely chosen lifestyle. Nevertheless one psychiatrist gave this definition: a homosexual is a heterosexual engaging in homosexual behavior. Whatever the origin and precise nature of this condition it will be the responsibility of the science of psychology to determine its true etiology. For those gays and lesbians who have freely chosen the homosexual lifestyle, one must understand that this is motivated in most cases by an addiction or obsession with disordered sex. While the homosexual tendency or orientation is also disordered, according to the Church it is not sinful. Homosexual behavior, whatever its origin, is a serious moral disorder, and in the judgment of the Church, it is also a grave sin.

The Catechism of the Catholic Church reminds us that the human person, not sexual orientation, identifies and defines each man and woman. Each person, despite any secondary conditions, must be respected. They must be treated with love and compassion despite any deficiencies. Nevertheless, homosexuality and lesbianism are threatening family life, and same sex marriages are being presented as a substitute for that important unit in society. Homosexual unions can never transmit life which is the principal purpose of marriage and family life. Same sex marriages are a perversion, for which decency in conduct, a study of the real nature and needs of every society, expert counseling, and the Ten Commandments are a highly recommended antidote.

Misused sex or lust has destroyed countless lives. Unfortunately, too many have not learned that sex and love, or lust and love, are not synonymous. Gays and lesbians, living together, have always been a distorted part of social life. These evils are prompted not only by the homosexual orientation but also by the desire to enjoy sex in this bizarre way. These social aberrations have plagued the great cultures of the past — Babylonian, Assyrian, Greek, Roman — and helped bring about their downfall. Now it has become a routine and expected part of the Judeo-Christian civilization and could lead the world into another cultural catastrophe. It must be acknowledged that sex addiction is a grave problem in our times.

The principal victims of this damaged culture, these broken homes and families, are the young and especially the children. From their earliest years they must contend with broken families and confusing suggestions and images that come into their life through television, radio, magazines and movies, and even the front rooms of their own homes, inviting them to follow the primrose path.

Day after day five great evils haunt our children, mostly because they lack a decent home life. Many of these children struggle alone with today's evil although they are seldom spiritually and morally prepared to do this. While each evil is distinct and separate, seldom are these found to be solitary evils.

VIOLENCE
The number of unborn infants being destroyed exceeds 1.5 million annually and is one of the worst examples of violence in our society. Tales of their casual and rou-

tine destruction are the subject of daily discussion. Those who survive life in the womb often witness violence between their own parents. Children, even infants, often suffer personal abuse from their own parents. This occurs long before they attend any school. Television, radio, movies, modern songs, continue to expose them to this form of evil from their earliest years. Every day we read about one of the latest problems — children killing children.

ALCOHOL
Another problem which often follows children from the front room of their own home is created by parents who drink to excess and always have plenty of liquor, wine, and beer available and on display. Some parents introduce their own young children to this destructive habit. If they escape this at home, studies show that many children are exposed to alcohol in elementary school and without a doubt in high school. The Columbia Study (CASA, 1997) reports that at least one million eighth graders admit to getting drunk each year. This recent study reports that 40 percent of those youth complaining of sexual harassment on dates blame the abuse of alcohol.

DRUGS
This is an evil that has become prevalent again in our times. There are 13 million cases of addictions currently. One in every twenty newborns already have drug addiction. In January 1997, 29.5% of 12 year olds reported having a friend or classmate who has used LSD, cocaine, or heroin, compared with 10.6% in 1996. For teens 12-17, the percentage jumped from 39% in 1996 to 56% in 1997. Children often become drug victims in elementary schools and spend the rest of their life struggling with this terrible and destructive problem.

SUICIDE
Six children commit suicide every day. In the last ten years this shattering event has increased one hundred percent. Many children believe they have no reason to live.

SEX
Recent studies reveal that many children at the age of eight are already entering puberty and that these youths at the rate of 7,700 a day become sexually active. 4,000 teens contract a sexually transmitted disease daily. Our children are having children. 1,000 teenage girls become pregnant every day. Approximately 2500 babies are born out of wedlock every day of the year. Every day 1100 children have abortions. Children are learning about the gay and lesbian lifestyle in school (designated as Programs in Diversity), often in programs presented by the public schools and approved by the Public School Board. The misuse and abuse of sex are destroying the lives of many grade and high schoolers regularly. Schools now provide teenagers with all the latest instruction, technology, and equipment needed for "safe sex" and

provide special education facilities where children can bring their babies while trying to finish school. What a tragedy for both mothers and children. This growing addiction to sex has been turned into one of the greatest destroyers of the lives of our children and youth.

The emphasis in this summary has been on current, specific, social problems. Nothing has been said regarding the great problems of basic philosophies which have developed over the years and which usually underlie these great problems. Modern philosophies are certainly doing their part to erode our culture and society. The list of these philosophies is lengthy: materialism, naturalism, personalism, secularism, hedonism, consumerism, scientism, and so on. There is an abundance of evidence that these philosophies have left their mark on our society. Indeed many of them are at the basis of the social problems mentioned. The social problems were emphasized because the public school philosophy deliberately notes that society and its "good" are the specific aims of its philosophy of education. The claim of public education is true; the result has been disastrous. In the meantime, the damage done to religion and religious values has been overwhelming.

The future of religious values in our nation is bleak. There is more hope for the improvement of our economy than there is for the improvement of our religious sense. Values have become "irrelevant, medieval, unnecessary, old-fashioned." Fornication and adultery have taken the place of the handshake. Even some of our own theologians are weakening sacred and fundamental traditions by trying to explain away the most basic teachings, duties, and obligations. Something must be done to save our youth, and the shortest path to the improvement of their spiritual and civic health is to repair the family. Strengthen the family and society can be saved.

So many wonderful things have happened in this century. Yet, in becoming so technologically and scientifically sophisticated, in making ourselves so modern, we have lost the real values. Now everything is relative; there are no absolutes. No longer can one point with the certainty we once enjoyed and say this is right, or this is wrong. It has been said that our highest standard of behavior today is often expressed in street language — "If it feels good, it's okay."

This is where education must play a special role. Schools have the task of keeping wisdom alive — the wisdom of the ages which includes the religious, moral and spiritual values that generations, centuries of people before us discovered, preserved and practiced for the good of society and themselves. Education must count among its first responsibilities keeping alive a sense of true religious and spiritual values.

"I regard hostility to religion in our schools as the greatest crime which I could commit against man or against God. Had I the power, I would sooner repeat the massacre of Herod then I would keep back religion from the young."[6] This extraordinarily strong statement comes from the pen of the dedicated "Father" of the Common School, Horace Mann.

Chapter 11 – Miscalculation

Let me tell you one more story about my grandfather. When I was a boy, we used to celebrate certain occasions in my grandfather's life. No, it was not his birthday. We celebrated grandfather's reception of the Holy Eucharist, which he did regularly twice a year with more solemnity than that of the Benedictine Monks installing a new Abbot. Twice a year was about par for Catholics who practiced the faith at the turn of the century.

On Saturday before Christmas and Easter my grandfather went to confession. He began to prepare for this early in the week. On Saturday afternoon he put on his best suit, his stiff collar and tie, and his nicely shined shoes. About seven o'clock in the evening he walked over a mile to the parish Church in order to go to confession. At the first Mass on Christmas and Easter he received Holy Communion. On Christmas and Easter morning, all his children and grandchildren were invited to his home for breakfast. There never was a breakfast like that: eggs, bacon, sausage, fried potatoes, my grandmother's fresh home-made rolls, bread and preserves — all we could eat. The important part came after breakfast.

On Christmas Day and on Easter Sunday the grandchildren were allowed to go into the "sacred" room in the house — my grandfather's meeting room, the parlor. He would lead us into the room and we removed the covers from the furniture and the drapes from the windows. Children and grandchildren would sit on the chairs and the floor around his famous marble table located in the middle of the room. It was like being in church. No one talked. As my grandfather sat at the marble table in the middle of the room, he would open the big book lying on the table, and read to us from the huge, ancient family Bible. That was the ceremony at my grandfather's house every Christmas and Easter. After about twenty minutes, which included a little sermonette, we were allowed to leave the parlor which was again shut tight. He gave a good little talk which really struck home. I remember how my parents, uncles, and aunts wiped the tears from their eyes as they left the room.

In our generation, the generation of my family, we did not have a parlor; we had a living room. I thought then and still think it was a much better arrangement. The room was used a lot more. The radio was to be found in the living room and later there was a television set. In our living room there was a card table against the wall which could easily be brought out and set up for a game at a moment's notice. Our family entertained a lot and it was all done in our living room. When friends came to visit we would sit around and talk, reminisce and laugh. It was a good room.

One important thing happened when we moved out of the parlor and opened the living room. In the new living room there was no convenient space for the marble table and the family Bible. My parents moved it into the adjourning hallway. When you came in the front door, there was a coat rack and next to it, the precious marble table. On the table in the hall was the family Bible. It wasn't too far away and it was still used. My dad and mother often read the Bible to us but more frequently they had one of the children read. The Bible was still a big part of our life.

The other day I visited my cousin's home with a definite mission in mind. My

Aunt Elizabeth, known affectionately as Aunt Lizzie, had died some years back and I could not remember the date. Fortunately, we made all those entries in the family Bible, and my cousin, the oldest of all the children in the family, had inherited the family Bible. Now I wanted to see it. I should warn you that my cousin does not have a parlor nor even a living room. She is a proud possessor of a den or a play room. There is no other room in the house that is occupied so completely and so frequently. This is where the family lives. Here is the stereo, the TV, family games, the bar, and this is where all the activity of the household, with or without guests, takes place.

I went into the den, and after a respectful delay, I asked to see the family Bible. I could have asked more successfully for the plans of the atomic bomb. The family Bible, they said, let's see — where would that be? It is here someplace, but we are not sure where. Then finally someone remembered that it was probably in the attic. That's where we found it.

Now this is a good family, what could be called an above average religious family, but even here the Bible has lost its privileged position in the home. It has gone from the center of the home to the attic.

What has happened to the family bible is a symbol of what has happened to religion, moral and spiritual values in the lives of Americans.

There are too many homes in America where the Bible has been taken out of the main room of the home and put out of the way into the attic.

The story of my grandfather relates something that has happened to our nation this past century. We have, so to speak, removed religious, moral, and spiritual values from the most important place in our lives, and put them into the attic of our life. All the while we were advancing in every other aspect of life, especially in science and technology.

It is one of the most important jobs of education to impart knowledge. It is also the most important job of education to discover, preserve, and impart parental and religious, spiritual, and moral values.

. . . . .

Our generation — our people and especially our children — need help. They have lost their way. They have lost an understanding of what is important, sacred, and truly meaningful in this life. They have lost any sense of responsibility about their own conduct and the conduct of others.

They no longer understand the meaning of and the purpose of restraint, self-control, and discipline. Many of them live simply as animals seeking pleasure wherever it may be found. The cost of all this has been tremendous. There is now hardly anything such as self-respect, self-worth, self-esteem, personal dignity, sensitivity to the needs of others. Seldom do we find anything resembling love or care for others

— an urge to reach out and help our brothers and sisters. There is neither love of God nor man — nor is there love of self. There is a wave of evil drowning us and we do not even recognize it as evil.

Our generation has developed a sense of indifference to evil. Few any longer accept it as a reality. Few can even identify it any more. We are all guilty. We must change our ways; we must show our youth how to live. We all must restore religion to a meaningful place in life. Especially the family must be restored. Broken homes and broken families are destroying all of us. Rebuild family life and society can regain its rightful place of dignity in our culture.

Chapter 11 — Miscalculation

NOTES

1) Oral tradition.

2) cf. *Newsweek,* Washington Post Company, New York, N. Y., Special Isssue, November 1997.

3) Vatican Council II, Church Today II, 57

4) The facts and statistics mentioned supplied by Department of Family Life Statistics, Allegheny County, Pa.

5) Rosetti, S. J. and, Coleman, G. D. , "Psychology and the Church's Teaching on Homosexuality," *America,* November, 1997, 6-23.

"Always Our Children", Statement of the Bishops' Committee on Marriage and Family, NCCB, October 1, 1997.

Harden, John F., S.J., observations on "Always Our Children."

Finnis, John, Letter on "Always Our Children", (Notre Dame, Indiana, October 28, 1997).

Catechism of the Catholic Church (Vatican Press, 1994), 2357-2359.

6) Dunn, William K., *Whatever Happened to Religious Education,* (Baltimore: John Hopkins Press, 1958), 172.

cf. Wade F. Horn, "Why There is no Substitute for Parents," *Imprimis,* Hillsdale College, Hillsdale, Michigan, June 1997.

National Center on Addiction and Substance Abuse (CASA), Columbia University Summer Research Study, 1997.

144

CHAPTER 12

Conclusion

"No Irish need apply" was a popular sign found in store fronts in the United States during the nineteenth century. It was not difficult to recognize the main target of this grass roots movement. It was, of course, the Catholics who were the object of this terrible bigotry. Some maintain that in reality the real target was the Catholic schools. Non-Catholic Americans had developed a real hatred for these schools, and such hatred did not abate when the signs were removed. This bigotry cut across every level of society and was deep seated. It was clear that Catholics and their schools were not welcome in this new country.

The signs do not appear any longer in our store windows chiefly because, as one prominent Catholic recently remarked, "We are now doing the hiring." Hopefully, if that is true, the hiring is being done in a kind, humane, and non-prejudicial way. Nevertheless, it would be wrong to think that the Catholic Church and her schools are no longer the object of a serious bigotry in this country. Bigotry and prejudice are well and alive.

There can be no doubt that anti-Catholicism had a dominant and decisive role in the establishment and development of the public school. Horace Mann hated the Catholic Church and said so clearly. He permitted only Protestants to participate in the early decisions about the nature of the Common School, especially about the role to be played by religion in its program. Catholics were not welcome. In the early efforts to reach a compromise allowing religion to serve education as church and parents desired, almost every state in the Union had developed some cooperative plan (cf. Chapter 1, 9; Chapter 11, 7). None survived.

Anti-Catholicism was intense throughout the nineteenth and well into the twentieth century, not only in the educational arena, but in the political and social realms as well. In Lemon v. Kurtzman, Justice Douglas, whom Justice Black joined in a negative decision, commented on this matter in a very interesting dictum:

> Early in the nineteenth century the Protestants obtained control of the New York school system and used it to promote reading and teaching of the Scriptures as revealed in the King James version of the Bible. The contest between Protestants and Catholics, often erupting into violence,

including the burning of Catholic Churches,, is a twice-told tale; the Know-Nothing Party, which included in its platform "daily Bible reading in the schools," carried three states in 1854 — Massachusetts, Pennsylvania and Delaware. Parochial schools grew and not Catholic schools alone. Other dissenting sects established their own schools — Lutherans, Methodists, Presbyterians and others. But the major force in shaping the pattern of education in this country was in the conflict between Protestants and Catholics. The Catholics logically argue that a public school was sectarian when it taught the King James version of the Bible. They therefore wanted it removed from the public schools; and in time they tried to get public funds for their own parochial schools.[1]

There was a continual attack on the Catholic Church and her schools, beginning with Horace Mann's refusal to allow Catholic representatives to discuss the role of religion in the common schools. Then came the violence involving fires destroying churches, threats against Sisters and their convents, the Know-Nothings, Grant's attack on "priestcraft," the Blaine Amendment, the infamous Oregon State Case, Al Smith's humiliating defeat for the presidency, and, of course, all this climaxed in the Everson and McCollum Cases. (cf. Chapter VIII). The existence of this bigotry and its influence on the school issue is' explicitly demonstrated in the dialogue between Justice Frankfurter and Attorney Franklin.[2] This conversation demonstrated, as did the court decisions, that anti-Catholicism was at the legal as well as the political roots of the school issue. The Everson and McCollum Cases prepared the way for Schempp; their conclusions tended to terminate not only the influence of Catholicism in American education, but would eventually exclude all religion from any possible involvement with public education.

This terrible history of bigotry in our nation has created at least two main problems for American society. The first of these problems was the involvement and commitment of the Supreme Court in the development of the public schools. The second was the need for an educational philosophy in the public school.

Bigotry came to a climax in the Supreme Court Case of 1925, Pierce v. Society of Sisters. The great question was: Can schools, other than public schools, operate legally in the United States? Under the leadership of the Scottish Rite Masons and assisted by the ku Klux Klan and other bigots, a statute was prepared requiring all children to fulfill State Compulsory Education Laws by attendance at public school only. Obviously, if this statute would stand, non-public schools could not meet the legal needs of parents and children. All children, then, would be compelled by law to attend public schools.

Fortunately the Supreme Court understood that it was not a mere question of public versus non-public schools. Rather it was a far greater question of parental rights versus state rights. What rights did parents have over the education of their children? How did states' rights compare to parental rights?

The Supreme Court announced the decision which should be fundamental and decisive in all American educational programs: "The child is not the mere creature of the state; those who nurture him and direct his destiny have the right, coupled with the high duty, to recognize him and prepare him for additional obligations."[3]

This historic decision settled a momentous question in American education, namely, the primacy of parental rights in determining the educational program of their children. The Constitution clearly maintains that the parental choice in selecting an elementary or secondary education supersedes any right which the state may have, and at the same time does not absolve the state from its obligation to provide education financially for these children.

The Supreme Court would subsequently dash the hopes of parents who wanted to direct the education of their children. This articulated right, so clearly based on the First Amendment, proved to be an empty promise — a mere privilege — and not a constitutional right so sacred in American life and law. If the primacy of parental rights in education had been maintained and properly pursued, the structure of American education would have been substantially different. So it was that the Supreme Court entered the educational picture as a key player.

It was noted that the Supreme Court defined the public school, its scope and its nature; consequently the Court, too, is responsible for American culture (cf. Introduction). Regrettably, the Supreme Court reneged on its decision in Pierce and clearly changed course on the matter of parental rights. By doing so the Court confirmed that the public schools were the official elementary and secondary educational institutions of the nation. Should parents exercise their choice — which Pierce had labeled primary — they would do so at their own expense. Their primary right of choice was merely an empty promise — a mere privilege.

Two subsequent decisions of the Supreme Court abandoned the course so properly chosen in the Pierce Case. Of course, many deny this claim. Parents, they say, can still select the school of their choice. But do they forget that now it is an empty choice? Without government financial help, that choice is meaningless.

In Everson (1947) and McCollum (1948) the hopes of Catholic and other parents were dashed by the affirmation that the parental choice was indeed meaningless. In both these cases new legislation was enacted by the Supreme Court by which the following things occurred. The Justices borrowed and canonized a metaphor from Thomas Jefferson's personal correspondence, written thirteen years after the approval of the First Amendment, and proclaimed it the official meaning of the First Amendment: "A wall of separation between Church and State." This was primarily the work of Justice Black. The real meaning of the First Amendment is, of course, that Congress shall not establish an official or national church or religion: the national government shall neither advance religion nor inhibit religion; all religions will receive equal treatment.

The concurring opinion of Justice Rutledge in the Everson Case is the most detailed attempt ever made to justify the position that the First Amendment means complete, absolute, irrevocable separation of religion from government.

Justice Rutledge in the Everson Case also erroneously states that the use of public monies to pay the cost of sectarian education would violate both the First Amendment and the specific statutory declaration involved, namely, "It is hereby declared to be the settled policy of the government to hereafter make no appropriation whatever for education in any sectarian school."

These principles established by both Justice Black and Justice Rutledge *have no foundation in constitutional law.* Rather they represent an invented legal means to continue a bitter bigotry and hatred against the Catholic Church and her schools.

An attempted neutralizing of the Catholic schools was not the final step in the Supreme Court's effort. Not only was Catholic religious involvement unwelcome in the public schools, but any attempt to make compromise plans to include Catholic and other religious instruction for public school students was consistently rejected. This contest finally ended with *the total elimination by the Supreme Court of all religious influence* — practices, devotions, or instructions — in public schools. This was accomplished by the Supreme Court in the notorious Schempp decision of 1963, 16 years after the Everson Decision.

Such respected, traditional, and venerable truths, highly prized by so many Americans, and so much a part of traditional education, were rejected as "garrulous absurdities," "false beliefs," and "organized superstitions" by statements of approval of the naturalistic philosophy of Dewey and his disciples, and by the Supreme Court through Schempp. Naturalism and secularism replace religion in the public school curriculum.

Justice Stewart, the lone dissenter on the Schempp decision, makes this thoughtful statement: "If religious exercises are held to be an impermissible activity in schools, religion is placed at an artificial and state-created disadvantage. Viewed in this light, permission of such exercises for those who want them is necessary if the schools are truly to be neutral in the matter of religion. And a refusal to permit religious exercises thus is seen, not as the realization of state neutrality, but rather as the establishment of a religion of secularism, or at least as government support of the beliefs of those who believe religious exercises should be conducted only in private."[4]

After 1850 Horace Mann's watered-down version of Protestantism became an even greater source of concern for Catholics and Protestants alike. The Catholics fought it; the Protestants gradually took over religion in the public school and strengthened it. This contest between Catholics and Protestants was very intense during the last half of the nineteenth century and the first part of the twentieth century.

Amidst this turmoil it was evident that the public school needed something to give meaning to its program. Needed was a philosophy of education. Enter John Dewey, a profound student and scholar of secular philosophy and a prolific writer. Dewey developed for the schools exactly what they wanted: a naturalistic and social philosophy to give purpose and cohesion to public education. Supernaturalism was totally repudiated.

Dewey began his mission as the philosopher for public education by presenting an article in *Naturalism and the Human Spirit,* denouncing as supernaturalism whatever is not scientifically tested. The final chapter in this symposium is by John Herman Randall, whose closing paragraph is a plea for faith in the empirical method.[5]

Dewey, more than any other person, gave the public schools a philosophy of education which was anti-supernatural and totally naturalistic, whose goals never exceeded the social.

The official American schools now had an official philosophy of education which would serve as the substratum for many teacher education programs and for every public elementary and secondary school educational program for the nation's children. It was not only non-sectarian (as was Horace Mann); it was totally godless and secular.

McClusky quotes Leo Pfeiffer (a lawyer representing the American Jewish Congress who fought intensely and tirelessly for a secular public school) from his book *Liberties of an American:* "The public schools must not only be non-sectarian but secular or godless."[6] This desire has now been realized fully, both because of decisions of the Supreme Court and because of the naturalistic, secularistic, godless, and social philosophy of John Dewey and his disciples, which clearly undergirds public school education.

Today the public schools — with numberless extraordinary buildings, outstanding teachers, brilliant administrators, countless consultants and staff in every area, a great variety of educational and co-educational programs, a seemingly unlimited supply of tax support, serving over 90% of the elementary and secondary school population — use none of these extraordinary advantages to give youth a share of the nation's rich spiritual and religious heritage. On the contrary, these resources are used to orient the child away from its religious and spiritual heritage by quietly, subtly, and often even directly and bluntly teaching the learner that the religious aspects of life are not worth their time, and implying clearly but unquestionably that the offered school programs alone are the only preparation necessary for life in the real world. The life so proposed is most often like the education provided — non-sectarian, godless and totally secular.

Parents, students, and others are informed without equivocation that religion cannot be taught, cannot inspire prayers or practices, because in our country it is forbidden to do so in public schools by the law of the land. Not getting involved in religion, not taking religion seriously, becomes a desirable and prudent goal for every growing American child. The results of these governmental decisions are clearly evident, as demonstrated in the previous chapter.

The results of this kind of education, powerfully presented by talented and sincere teachers and administrators year after year, are now clearly evident. Children are taught the emptiness of religion — and religion is ignored in the individual and social life of most of them. The Commandments are not allowed to be displayed, let alone taught. And recently the Department of Education[7] found 116,000 "incidents" of theft and 98,000 of vandalism. "Among more serious crimes" the study reports about 4,000 rapes a year, 7,000 robberies, and 11,000 fights or attacks with weapons. Within days new bills, with billions of dollars, were sent to Congress to intensify studies, hire more teachers, and lower class size.

What is hurting education cannot be corrected by throwing more money at the schools. It is time that some honest admissions be made and that real problems be faced.

If anything is overdue it is the repair of the broken family and the destroyed children who are the products of those broken families. The sacredness of the family, our family values, our religious ideals and heritage, must somehow be put back into action.

As for those parents who wish to have an education for their children which excels in "non-sectarianism, secularism, and godlessness," let all know that such an education is already available and is being generously and handsomely provided by the government in its official schools. It is producing overwhelming results.

The supreme law of our land as expressed in the Pierce v. Society of Sisters v. Pierce requires that all parents choose the kind of education which they desire for their children. It does not say that this choice must be at their own expense. This, indeed, can include, as it once did in public education, religion and the teachings of their church as well as the required school subjects. This choice deserves a positive response from the government — and not a meaningless, empty recognition of the right to choose the kind of school parents desire, but also the right to financial support by their government for the school of choice.

There can be no doubt that such changes in the school program will take time. Until the Constitution can be properly explained and implemented, vouchers for the school of choice should be issued to parents of those children who have chosen another form of education.

These are critical times. Our culture is gradually being destroyed by a vicious attack on family life and therefore on our society. Divorce, single parent families, homosexuality, same-sex "marriages," adultery, fornication, murder, alcohol, drugs, violence, the media, pre-marital and extra-marital promiscuous sex, hedonism, consumerism, materialism, secularism imperil our culture by direct attacks on families, youth, and society. Parents and youth need help.

The negative presentation of religion resulting from the direct and official policy of our public schools, the exclusion of religion from the lives of our school youth in every official school activity, is being accomplished at a tremendous cost to our children, our families, and our society. Religious instruction and practices could bring some immediate relief to this evil situation. Secularism and godlessness are destroying us. Must the history of other great cultures be repeated, or will we find the courage to do what must be done?

Chapter 12 — Conclusion

The Federal Government is the final resource for seeking an answer to these problems. The future of our children, our families, our nation — the survival of our culture and civilization — depend to a great extent on the Federal Government's involvement and response, not its neutrality.

- Something must be done to replace John Dewey's secularism and natural-ism as the official "religion" and philosophy of our public schools. True religious family values must be acknowledged and taught.

- Something must be done to support those educational programs which, while providing an education in state required secular subjects, also pro-vide the child with religious and spiritual knowledge, attitudes, values, ideals, and practices, thus preparing youth for a complete and full life in this world and beyond.

- Something must be done by the public school authorities to encourage and to implement cooperative religious education programs, such as that struck down by McCollum, so that religious programs will be available, freely chosen, convenient, friendly, and will make religion a recognized part of the public school program if any good is to be accomplished. Those who instruct in these special, regularly scheduled, officially recog-nized classes in religion must be the choice of parents as well as approved by the state, and teach in public classrooms.

- Something must be done to restore our culture to its intended direction: this can be accomplished by restoring the true meaning of our Constitution; by recognizing the role of religion in education; and by acknowledging the rights of all parents and all children in American society.

- Parents selecting other schools must have that choice honored and finan-cially supported. No penalties for exercising this constitutional choice can be tolerated.

Implementation of these proposals will involve significant change. Fortunately that is precisely what the philosophy of John Dewey and his disciples vigorously maintained to be the main ingredient of public school philosophy — change. These changes will be, we believe, for the good of the public schools. They will relieve an oppressive monopolistic educational system by introducing and encouraging real competition; they will respond to the constitutional demands of parents who seek and support such changes; they will permit the restoration of a dynamic philosophy of education which fostered the establishment of our first public schools and thus allow the revival of religious, spiritual, and moral values.

Chapter 12 — Conclusion

· · · · ·

In the opening lines of this brief study it was proposed that three factors played a particularly important although not exclusive role in fashioning the present state of American culture.

One of the most fundamental is public education. Seldom has anything played a more influential role in the development of a nation and its culture than its educational program. One is tempted to compare this influence today with the role formerly played by religion up through the ages to the enlightenment.

In addition to the influence of public education, Catholic education also plays a minor yet a not insignificant role. Its influence has also been studied in the preceding pages.

Finally, an unexpected yet real influence has been the Supreme Court, and no study of the nation's educational program or its culture would be complete without examining this important factor. The Supreme Court's influence on our society in general, and especially education, has been substantial if not extraordinary.

Culture concerns our way of life — what we think of life and how we actually live it. Culture also identifies those qualities of life that we believe should be preserved and are worthy to pass on to the next generation. While one hopes that culture shows us at our very best, often it merely demonstrates what we perceive or at least hope to be our very best.

No doubt education is one of the most influential designers of culture. It demonstrates, perhaps more clearly than anything else, what a people claim as valuable — worthy of their effort — deserving of their aspirations and hopes: those things they wish to pass on to the next generation. Some things become important in our culture because through them people accomplish what they consider to be great or significant. Thus, we hope our culture demonstrates our values and our aspirations at their very best. This is often only a hope.

Regrettably, public education, which is perhaps the greatest designer of culture in every generation, has sold out some of the key ideals and values which once gave it meaning. Religion, for example, always considered an integral part of every culture throughout history, has been sold short. Its role no longer equals that of public education and therefore it is minimized in the development and design of American culture. It is no longer considered an indispensable part of the American way of life, or our values and our aspirations. Now we can do without religion — and many people do just that.

To complicate this matter, the Supreme Court, whose constitutional role is to interpret the nation's laws and to be concerned with maintaining and operating the judiciary processes, has now assumed the role of lawmaker. In recent years it has

152

taken on this deliberate role, through its own creation of laws, to determine the form and nature of public education. This has seriously affected our culture. In case after case it has attempted to define what American education should be and what essentially should be involved in it or excluded from it.

Religion has been its first victim. Always an integral part of American education, and education in general, religion has been clearly bypassed by the Supreme Court. The Court has not only denied that it is a right of every American to be educated in religion, but has clearly stated that religion will receive no moral or financial assistance from the nation's tax funds. The very survival of religion has been threatened; its need has been challenged. The Supreme Court has also proclaimed as a national policy that religion is to be clearly separated forever from any and all government affairs.

In the meantime, through the inestimable and heavily supported efforts of public education, specific subjects have taken on greater importance in our life and now are used to define its meaning. Where religion once stood, there now is science, technology, the development of new philosophies, such as naturalism, evolutionism, hedonism, and materialism. Supernaturalism has been excluded from any significant place in life or in our way of life. Religion is simply ignored generally in American life.

From our point of view the results have been disastrous. The present and future of our culture, we believe, will be bleak. If men seek to answer the questions and mysteries of life in this restricted way, we are indeed in great trouble. If the guidance of religion is ignored we are indeed the most of all people to be pitied. There is a small, promising light still flickering — weakly but dimly — which might restore to our culture a hope of reaching our aspirations and potential. It is Catholic education. Perhaps in the words of the Vatican Council that dim light may still result in a "growth in the human spirit, ability to wonder, to understand, to contemplate, to make personal judgments, and to develop (our) religious, moral and social sense."

Yes, public education does influence our culture — and so does the Supreme Court — for better or worse. Thank God, so does Catholic education — when it can.

NOTES

1) Lemon v. Kurtzman (I 970), 89, U.S.

2) Supra, Chapter IX, 166.

3) Pierce v. Society of Sisters (1925), 268, U.S. 150.

4) Schempp, 374 U.S. 203, 313

5) Vincent Edward Smith, *Idea Men of Today,* (Milwaukee, Bruce, 1950), 25.

6) McClusky, 130, **cf** note

7) Reported in the *Pittsburgh Post Gazette,* Wednesday, March 25, 1998, A-7.